The Librarian's Guide to Bibliotherapy

ALA Editions purchases fund advocacy, awareness,
and accreditation programs for library professionals worldwide.

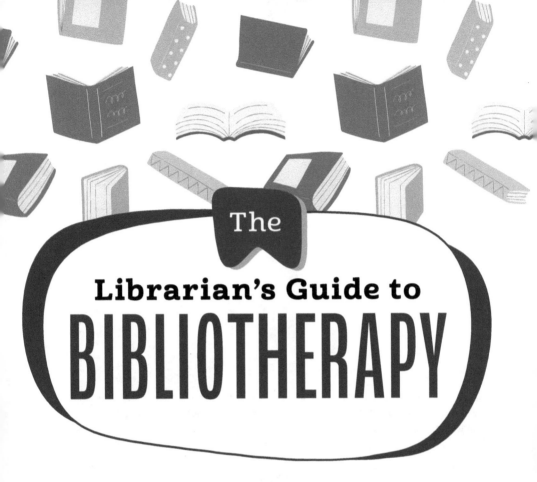

The
Librarian's Guide to
BIBLIOTHERAPY

JUDIT H. WARD and NICHOLAS A. ALLRED

ALA Editions
CHICAGO | 2024

Extensive effort has gone into ensuring the reliability of the information in this book; however, the publisher makes no warranty, express or implied, with respect to the material contained herein.

ISBN: 978-0-8389-3662-7 (paper)

Library of Congress Cataloging-in-Publication Data

Names: Ward, Judit Hajnal, 1959- author. | Allred, Nicholas A., 1991- author.
Title: The librarian's guide to bibliotherapy / Judit H. Ward and Nicholas A. Allred.
Description: Chicago : ALA Editions, 2024. | Includes bibliographical references and index. | Summary: "The bibliotherapy-informed practices, programs, and events outlined in this guide will help librarians support the mental health and personal growth of their patrons"—Provided by publisher.
Identifiers: LCCN 2023027539 | ISBN 9780838936627 (paperback)
Subjects: LCSH: Libraries—Activity programs. | Bibliotherapy.
Classification: LCC Z716.33 .W37 2023 | DDC 025.5—dc23/eng/20230815
LC record available at https://lccn.loc.gov/2023027539

Book design by Alejandra Diaz in the Cabrito Sans, Cabrito and Expo Serif Pro typefaces.

♾ This paper meets the requirements of ANSI/NISO Z39.48-1992 (Permanence of Paper).

Printed in the United States of America

28 27 26 25 24   5 4 3 2 1

CONTENTS

Contents

PREFACE

A clinical psychologist walks into the library . . .

The idea of this book can be traced back to a reference interaction that happened almost two decades ago. A practicing clinical psychologist-researcher walked into the Center of Alcohol Studies Library at Rutgers, the State University of New Jersey, to collect reading material to complement her treatment program for couples. Little did we know that this moment—followed by joint research on the potential of bibliotherapy to complement the treatment of substance use disorder—would lead to the first-ever recovery-themed bibliotherapy project, and it would later expand into various reading programs to promote wellness in diverse settings.

It was a tall order for the new librarian. The first alcohol studies collection in the world, the Center of Alcohol Studies Library maintained one of the world's largest and most comprehensive collections of English-language documents pertaining to the biomedical and psychosocial aspects of substance use, mostly scholarly publications, until its closure in December 2016. A small part of this library was a special section featuring fiction, memoirs, biographies, and similar genres, called the Alcohol-NJ collection, sponsored by the state of New Jersey. But then a happy accident took place after weeding the reference collection. A large shelf space became available in a central area in the library, and this became the new home of Alcohol-NJ. Moving these nonscholarly titles to a more central location changed the way that users interacted with them, as these shelves were both prominent enough to invite browsing and private enough for self-conscious users not to feel watched. That privacy was particularly important—simply being seen looking through these titles might feel embarrassing for users grappling with the social stigma surrounding their own or loved ones' addictions, and librarians might wind up in reference interactions that quickly became more fraught and personal than they might feel equipped to handle. Privacy helped, but it was only the first of many new considerations for our academic library as we started leveraging our collections for readers' emotional and therapeutic needs as well as their intellectual ones.

In short, we found that addressing therapeutic motivations for reading—an aspect that academic libraries in particular tend not to think about very often—thrust us into the role of "accidental bibliotherapists," performing a kind of readers' advisory that our previous reference experience and training had not prepared us for. The reference infrastructure for such interactions was not there either. When that psychologist asked for a booklist on couples therapy and addiction issues, we quickly discovered that no such booklist existed—not on that topic, nor many others with a practical, therapeutic bent. We knew we had the books to help, that the books were out there that could offer counsel and comfort for almost any reader in need. The difficulty was in connecting those books to the readers who needed them.

With a strong belief in the transformative potential of reading, we developed a program called "Reading for Recovery" to help fellow librarians better serve patrons without laying claim to psychiatric expertise. Funded through a Carnegie–Whitney Grant from the American Library Association, the pilot project in 2015/16 gathered material to assist "accidental bibliotherapists" when patrons asked for reading recommendations. The project envisioned reading and/or group discussion as a supplement to, not a substitute for, recovery programs and more traditional forms of therapeutic support. In the next few years, it was followed by many other guided reading programs and bibliotherapy-inspired projects, big and small, geared toward broader audiences.

An uplifting experience inspired us to do more when we were swept away by the power of a tight-knit community with trust in a safe, non-judgmental environment. In 2016 at the joint conference of the Substance Abuse Librarians and Information Specialists and the Association of Mental Health Librarians in Denver, we shared the accomplishments of Reading for Recovery in a short demo followed by a workshop. In a conference room decorated with a series of posters related to our project, we discussed a personal but relatively safe topic—insomnia—through one of our staple short stories. Sharing their own experiences openly and recommending reading material to each other for various scenarios, librarians were not only thrilled to participate but, judging by the questions and comments during and after the presentation, many of them also felt inspired to start their own programs. Inspiration goes both ways; we also felt more motivated by our colleagues, both by their enthusiastic participation and by their suggested further applications of these methods.

We are honored to share our experiences and ideas in this handbook. The intention is to inspire and empower librarians in all settings, in public, academic, special, and school libraries, who are planning to explore an innovative use of their existing collections for the purpose of guided reading for mental health. It is not a book that you have to read cover to cover. Instead, we recommend reading short passages and reflecting on what you read: Would this work in my library? How can I implement a similar program? How can I tweak this method? Where should I start? In other words, what might you learn from our story before writing your own?

We hope to inspire you just as reading and discussing texts with our users inspired and motivated us to collect and share our thoughts in this book.

ACKNOWLEDGMENTS

The authors are grateful for family, friends, and loved ones who provided support in bringing this book into the world. Particular thanks are due to the staff of the former Center of Alcohol Studies Library, where this bibliotherapy journey first began. We also want to thank the guest contributors who lent their expertise to this book: part of embracing the status of "accidental bibliotherapist" involves recognizing the limits of one's own knowledge, and we are grateful for the colleagues in these pages who have made this book more rich and complete than we could have made it ourselves. Last and most of all, we want to thank our editor, Jamie Santoro, for her early and unwavering support and her always perceptive feedback. Our hope for this book is to have come close to the best version of itself, which Jamie has always seemed to have in her mind's eye; what we know for sure is that without her, it would not exist at all.

INTRODUCTION

Why Bibliotherapy

Bibliotherapy, or the use of guided reading for therapeutic purposes, is not a new concept. One could argue that bibliotherapy goes all the way back to Aristotle's *Poetics* in 335 BCE, which claims that tragedies allow spectators to experience and release difficult feelings in a controlled environment—a process he termed catharsis. If this is the ancestor of contemporary bibliotherapy, it's come a long way since then: in recent times, bibliotherapy has been used to help treat disorders including insomnia, anxiety, obsessive compulsive disorder, and addiction, and it has shown promise in studies for both children and adults. There is a significant variety in the forms bibliotherapy can take, from a healthcare setting under the supervision of a doctor or counselor to lightly guided or entirely self-directed courses of therapeutic reading. This book will show through best practices and brief case studies how you can apply bibliotherapy's insights—that books can help readers process difficult emotions and navigate life's challenges—to create inclusive, rewarding, and sustainable programs for your library that fulfill its mission to serve its community.

Whether we recognize it or not, librarians often become "accidental bibliotherapists" (to borrow Liz Brewster's apt term) when providing book recommendations and readers' advisory to a patron or running book discussions, either in person or online. This book seeks to acknowledge the work that librarians already do—as well as the practical limits of that work for the vast majority of librarians who are not licensed mental health professionals—and offer bibliotherapy-informed ideas for library-based reading programs that draw on the skills librarians already have.

Bibliotherapy in the Library

The library isn't just a quiet place to read or use a computer—it's also a pillar of the local community and a hub of diversity, equity, and inclusion efforts. Libraries serve patrons of all backgrounds and seek to provide information and resources to all who need it without bias or prejudice. The library is also a safe space, providing programs that foster discussions in a nonthreatening, nonjudgmental environment, even on sensitive topics of community concern. As a framework for thinking about this aspect of the library's work more broadly—helping connect patrons of all backgrounds with meaningful reading and dialog on the topics that matter most to them—bibliotherapy fits the modern library's mission like a glove.

Library-based programs inspired by bibliotherapy practices promise to engage users, showcase collections, raise the library's profile, and serve the community. Moreover, at a time when libraries are particularly interested in fostering diversity, equity, and inclusion, bibliotherapy programs are a perfect fit: being free of charge makes library-based guided reading programs already inherently inclusive and equitable, and they can allow libraries to address the needs and concerns of marginalized communities, highlight holdings that allow patrons from underrepresented backgrounds to see themselves reflected in literature, and expose all patrons to new perspectives.

This book aims to help librarians take the step beyond advising patrons, to designing and implementing bibliotherapy-informed programs with confidence and tested strategies. When properly executed, guided reading initiatives mirror the core values of the library and further its mission, whether by responding to emerging local needs, highlighting diverse collection offerings, or providing a free and intrinsically equitable open-access resource to the community.

How This Book Will Help

As a librarian, you should feel empowered in the important role of connecting books with readers. Librarians have already sought to develop their collections based on the needs of their users. Many titles already lined up on the shelves of your library are perfectly suitable for bibliotherapy-inspired programs. With a little guidance provided here, it's worth a try to make them more discoverable and available for those who can benefit from them the most when they need them the most. Ideas in this book aim to assist librarians who want to mobilize their collections for new programs and outreach efforts.

Are you worried about lacking the expertise necessary to launch a guided reading project? Librarians are already equipped with many transferable skills required to experiment with new projects and create a successful bibliotherapy program in the long run. Think of some of the things you may be doing already: providing readers' advisory, familiarizing yourself with the collection, knowing your users, and promoting the library and its programs (including social media). You're already most of the way there!

As that description also indicates, librarians are busy and sometimes stretched thin already. Luckily, there's no need to reinvent the wheel. This practical handbook offers sample programs, best practices, and templates and guidelines for how to leverage your library's existing collections and resources for your new programs and outreach initiatives. The book presents versions and alternatives that can be easily adapted to your local library environment and tailored to your target audience.

WRITE THE BOOK YOU WANT TO READ

The great novelist Toni Morrison famously said, "If there's a book that you want to read, but it hasn't been written yet, then you must write it." When we launched our first bibliotherapy-inspired program called "Reading for Recovery," there was no book available for librarians on how to start a bibliotherapy program in a library. The scholarship available at that time focused on clinical rather than library settings. As we developed our collection and continued with other projects, we kept looking for ideas on how to grow, but still couldn't find a book written with our situation in mind. Thus, we decided to follow Toni Morrison's advice, and the result is this book: all the guidelines, pointers, and encouragement that we wish we'd had at the outset of our bibliotherapy-inspired journey.

How to Read This Book: Fixed Menu or Buffet

As with most handbooks, you can choose how you want to engage with this book: you're welcome either to read it cover to cover or simply to consult individual chapters for ideas that will provide answers to your most pressing questions. Organized around practical steps, each chapter starts with an overview of its full content and ends with the takeaway "In a Nutshell." Real-life examples and stories in text boxes will prompt you to reflect on the chapter while providing further information and inspiration. Templates in various chapters and in the appendixes offer material that you can tailor to your own setting.

Getting Acquainted

Part I gives an overview of bibliotherapy: the concept, its history, and different approaches to it today. Chapter 1 summarizes the distinction between clinical bibliotherapy—undertaken as part of a prescribed treatment, often featuring nonfiction self-help materials—and developmental bibliotherapy, which involves a broader view of therapeutic reading outside the clinical setting. Chapter 2 walks you through a few milestones in the history of bibliotherapy via vignettes of pioneering bibliotherapists, including some of their own words. This part will get you up to speed on what bibliotherapy looks like today, introduce theoretical models to understand the process, and hopefully inspire you to consider bibliotherapy-adjacent guided reading programs in your own library.

Turning Inward

If you fail to plan, you plan to fail, as the saying goes. Before getting started—before even taking baby steps—you may want to do a bit more than just a little soul searching. Part II presents components and options for bibliotherapy-inspired programming for you to begin. Chapter 3 walks you through the basic steps to factor in once you have set your vision and come up with your concept, such as your financial situation, the available skills, your allies, and timing, and how to put all these into practice reinventing yourself as an accidental bibliotherapist! Chapter 4 reviews potential options from "passive programming" such as book displays, reading lists, read-alikes, and web resources to more active initiatives. Comparing them to what you are already doing, this chapter also guides you to complement your existing practice, such as incorporating a bibliotherapy focus to your one-on-one readers' advisory consultations. Chapter 5 focuses on how to tailor your program to your audiences, offering examples and scenarios.

Getting to Work

So, you've decided to bring insights from bibliotherapy to your library. When it's time to test the waters, part III is here to help! Instead of jumping into the pool in the deep end, you may want to start small. You already know a lot about book selection and matching a book with a reader. Chapter 6 focuses on how to select reading material for your audience with bibliotherapy in mind. Chapters 7 and 8 go into detail on the two most popular and visible programming methods: group discussions and large public events, respectively. Both chapters compare bibliotherapy-inspired programs to the kind of programming you already offer in your library, showing how you can build on your skills and experience. Part III will reassure you that implementing bibliotherapy-inspired programming in your library is well within reach!

Turning Outward

If your program is not on social media, it's not happening, right? Marketing and assessment are important elements of any program in the library. They both, however, add to the workload of librarians. Chapter 9 recommends thinking about marketing early and often as you plan your program, and it offers tips, tools, and branding ideas to make the most of your resources and effectively find your audience. Social media gets its own turn in the spotlight in Chapter 10: it can be fun, but it's also important to recognize as work and plan for actively! Chapter 11 helps demystify SMART goals, which are broken down in the context of bibliotherapy-inspired projects in the library. There's no single recipe for a successful program, and the proof is in the pudding—building in assessment tools from the beginning will allow you to taste-test and tweak your program at every stage to achieve the results you want. Along with synergies with existing programs and templates we advocate in various places in the book, this chapter will help you focus on improving and sustaining your bibliotherapy-inspired projects.

Looking Forward

The final chapter features new areas for exploration and experimentation. Therapeutic reading is just the proverbial tip of the iceberg: once you've started to facilitate the kind of personal development and growth that reading can provide, why not expand to related pursuits like creative writing, visual art, and more? Our farewell chapter is meant to encourage you to not only put into practice what you take away from this book, but also take your programs into new directions that fit your own library and community. You may find yourself developing as well, personally and professionally.

ENTERING THE GLASS CASTLE

When we received our first query on reading material suitable for addictions bibliotherapy, we dug into our circulation metrics and discovered that certain nonacademic books in the collection were checked out way more often than others in this academic library! The most frequently circulating title was *The Glass Castle* by Jeannette Walls, a memoir "about the author's unconventional, poverty-stricken upbringing at the hands of eccentric, nomadic parents, one a frustrated artist and the other a brilliant alcoholic," as summarized in "R4R @ Rutgers: Reading for Recovery," our first bibliotherapy-themed guide. There was a clear interest in stories that reflected people's experiences with substance use disorders.

The logical approach was to get way out of our comfort zone and look into readers' advisory—a practice familiar in public libraries, far less familiar in academic libraries like ours. The reading lists we created for in-house use served as the basis for Reading for Recovery, our ALA-funded bibliotherapy project. That project, in turn, eventually led us to writing this book. It all started with a single query and a surprising finding about our circulation that indicated an unexpected need among our users. We hope that bibliotherapy leads you in exciting new directions as well!

It All Adds Up

Although this book is the brainchild of an academic librarian and English literature professor, it should be noted that contributions received from readers and program participants, consciously or accidentally, have been considered, incorporated, and greatly appreciated. This book is an example of how to engage a variety of people, embrace diverse opinions, and respond to evolving needs such as reading for wellness, to create something meaningful. Our own journey followed a route from specific to more general; yours can take any direction, turn, or zigzag.

Bibliotherapy as You Do It

Do these activities all really fall under bibliotherapy? Well, yes and no. Very few librarians are certified to run counseling sessions. But we are perfectly qualified to select reading material for the library collection to meet our patrons' needs; make book recommendations based on a readers' advisory interview; organize a book club for targeted groups; host a large public event (even on a shoestring budget); and document, assess, and promote all these activities for our patrons, library administration, and stakeholders.

A Job Well Done Is Its Own Reward

Working with people—adults and children alike—and watching them grow is very rewarding as they take on the journey to becoming a better self, a better version of themselves, whether in a bibliotherapy group setting or among coworkers working on the bibliotherapy project. We have experienced how the process made an impact on our own lives, helping us through difficult phases, from a library closure to new beginnings, professional crisis and personal loss, even a global pandemic. Helping others helped us cope, and we hope it will do the same for you. Alongside the material benefits mentioned above, reading and sharing books with others can be a rewarding, transformative experience in its own right—indeed, bibliotherapy itself is all about taking that personally transformative aspect of reading seriously. We hope you'll find as much fulfillment and joy in sharing bibliotherapy with your patrons as we have with ours.

LANGUAGE AND BIBLIOTHERAPY

A note on the language used for guided reading and in this book. Librarians are familiar with the challenges of communicating ideas to all patrons, colleagues, and stakeholders without sounding omniscient and patronizing. Language use is a significant component of creating an environment for everyone to feel safe and inspired to speak up. A book is not any different. We have tried to use inclusive and empowering language in this book to the best of our ability. In particular, we want to be transparent about our direct address to "you," the reader, throughout the book: we chose this approach in order to make readers feel welcome. This book is meant for all who can use it, in whatever way they see fit.

PART I

Getting Acquainted

01 Bibliotherapy: An Overview

Ever been on edge (maybe even recently)? If you feel less grumpy after some alone time with your favorite book, congratulations! You've just experienced the basic mechanism of bibliotherapy: the salutary effects of reading on mental health. Pondering about plots, characters, and texts in general will not only distract you, but, with some guidance, it can help you reflect on what's happening in the book and what's happening to you—which ultimately will help you develop your own tools to better handle whatever life throws your way.

This chapter is a brief introduction to the theory and various practices of bibliotherapy. It will lay a foundation so that you—someone who has no doubt experienced the therapeutic effects of reading and has perhaps been thrust into the role of an "accidental bibliotherapist"—can more intentionally facilitate therapeutic encounters with books for your patrons and community members.

What Is Bibliotherapy?

An umbrella term, bibliotherapy refers to an array of practices that use reading to support mental, emotional, and even physical health. A drug-free auxiliary-treatment method, bibliotherapy typically involves patients reading books or other texts from a list created under the guidance of a subject expert to address a therapeutic need. Although the practice has received growing attention in recent years, the term itself was first coined over a century ago; the underlying belief that books can provide healing benefits to readers is one that dates all the way back to antiquity.

The definitions of *bibliotherapy* tend to swing to one of the two directions expressed in the two parts of the compound noun: *biblio* + *therapy*. From Greek *biblion*, meaning "book," the prefix *biblio* relates to books and, by extension, refers to literature. According to the *Oxford English Dictionary*, *therapy* originates from the modern Latin *therapia* and the Greek *therapeia* and means "healing."

On the "biblio" end of the seesaw, some guided reading for therapeutical or wellness purposes uses only traditional literary works, such as fiction, poetry, and drama. Therapists in this group accept only "high literature," limiting their selection of possible readings to works of established literary authors. Grounded not only in psychotherapy, but also in literary theory and analysis, these sessions focus on a single text at a time. The therapist guides the conversation as dictated by individual or group needs. This type is often called *creative bibliotherapy* or *developmental bibliotherapy*. By contrast, at the "therapy" end, *bibliotherapy* can refer to any use of reading material distributed by healthcare professionals to complement treatment—sometimes called *clinical bibliotherapy*. This typically involves self-help publications prescribed by a trained healthcare professional.

Approaches to Books That Heal

It would require an entire book to take stock of the various approaches to bibliotherapy across different disciplines—and this isn't that book. Our main focus here is helping you find and implement an approach that's right for your library! In lieu of that more comprehensive account of the different varieties of bibliotherapy, here's a quick overview of two main approaches:

Clinical Bibliotherapy

The term *clinical bibliotherapy* refers to the use of mostly nonfiction reading material that healthcare professionals such as psychologists, licensed therapists, and clinical social workers recommend to their patients to complement in-person treatment, often as a part of ongoing cognitive behavioral therapy. The material would typically be a self-help publication, a brochure, or a workbook, which might or might not be accompanied by another textbook-type publication. Examples include therapy manuals and workbooks from reputable authors and publishers, available in public libraries or for purchase. The use of self-help texts is sometimes referred to as self-help bibliotherapy.

Developmental Bibliotherapy

Developmental bibliotherapy typically involves guided reading of traditional literary works, such as fiction, poetry, or drama. Conducted by bibliotherapists trained in psychotherapy as well as literary theory and analysis, sessions discuss a single text at a time—a single poem or short story. During a session, the therapist usually reads the text aloud and guides the conversation as dictated by the needs of the individual or group. Group therapy rules apply, such as confidentiality, privacy, and appropriate behavior. In the case where the bibliotherapy group operates as a book club, titles are selected by the librarian or group leader, and participants are expected to read the book before the meeting. A variety of support materials can make these sessions more manageable and successful, such as discussion questions, talking points, or a list of books for special conditions.

BIBLIOTHERAPY BY DISCIPLINE

Another way to compare approaches to guided reading is by the field from which they originate: library and information science or psychology, focusing on different aspects as listed below. Both library- and psychology-based bibliotherapy are interested in facilitating personal growth, and both connect reading to healing; the difference is a matter of emphasis: the library-based approach tends to conceive of the client primarily as a *reader*, whereas the psychology-based approach tends to conceive of the client primarily as a *patient*. This distinction can be seen, for example, in the choice of reading material. A patient-centered approach treats the reading as a supplemental tool to bring about a treatment, and so it might include nonfiction or self-help workbooks that offer clients direct advice (rather than inviting literary analysis). By contrast, a reader-centered approach is primarily concerned with keeping clients intellectually and aesthetically engaged, and so would be likely to include works of literature that could provoke an interesting discussion despite—or perhaps because of—their lack of a clear message or therapeutic "prescription." In this approach, the reading, thinking, and discussing *are* the prescription.

TABLE 1.1

Reader-Centered and Patient-Centered Bibliotherapy Compared

Reader-centered bibliotherapy	Patient-centered bibliotherapy
The reading, thinking, and discussing are the "prescription"	The reading delivers or reinforces the "prescription"
Modeled on a seminar or book club	Modeled on individual or group psychotherapy
May include works of literary interest without a direct or explicit therapeutic takeaway	May include works with a direct or explicit therapeutic takeaway that are not intended for literary analysis
Emphasis is on engagement with the text	Emphasis is on personal application of the text
Tends to be developmental (but can be clinical)	Tends to be clinical (but can be developmental)

Adapted from Judit Béres, "Reading for Recovery: Person-Centered Biblio-therapy," poster presented at the 38th Annual Conference of the Substance Abuse Librarians and Information Specialists, Denver, CO, May 4–7, 2016.

Informal Bibliotherapy

In an especially casual form of "bibliotherapy," perhaps better termed simply reading therapy, online forums present opportunities for book lovers to discuss and recommend titles to each other that have helped them deal with an issue. Lists such as "10 Books That Will Help You Manage Your Anxiety Today!" pop up daily and claim to provide comfort or relief by means of escapism. Diverse choices run the gamut from *The Bell Jar* to *The Lord of the Rings*, making it difficult to authenticate the relevance and benefit of individual titles without reading them for oneself.

Why are these nonetheless valuable? Firsthand testimonials in a safe environment, on a forum of like-minded peers, can be very powerful. Reading about similar feelings and issues might help the reader identify their own and feel encouraged and motivated to seek help. Most important, the experience might also bring about the feeling that one is "not alone," that others are sharing a similar experience. Discovering through a memoir that the reader shares a mental health issue with a celebrity, for instance, is different than just escaping from the real world; it's a way of reframing their own struggles by seeing those struggles reflected in someone else.

The mere existence of these sites indicates not only the need but also a shift from rigorous clinical bibliotherapy to broader areas such as literature, both poetry and fiction. In addition to case studies, randomized controlled trials, and systematic reviews, bibliotherapy can be considered as an upcoming field better positioned for multidisciplinary qualitative and mixed-method research. The perceptible shift in bibliotherapy from self-help to shelf help provides exciting, new opportunities for librarians, who can turn to their collections stocked with remedies.

What's missing from "everyday" bibliotherapy? It's the "guided" component of guided reading: you, the expert who can select titles for any given topic or issue available in the local collection. Whether in the solitary work of compiling curated reading lists, displays, guides, and talking points to reflect on, or the more public-facing role of organizing programs to connect with existing patrons and groups in the larger community, librarians are uniquely well prepared to provide the guidance to facilitate therapeutic reading. While it's important to keep in mind the qualifications we librarians are unlikely to have—clinical training and expertise in mental health care—we also have both literary and organizing skills that are a natural fit for these kinds of programs.

Bibliotherapy and Librarians

As an information services rather than a mental health professional, you may be feeling apprehensive about attempting something with the word therapy in its name. That worry is perfectly understandable, and even healthy: it's important to recognize the limits of your own expertise. We do not advocate that you practice psychotherapy through libraries unless you're separately qualified for that kind of work.

Instead, we want to highlight the aspects of therapeutic reading that are *already present* in library practice and show you how to implement guided reading programs with therapeutic reading in mind. If you've ever done a readers' advisory related to a patron's personal concern, or if you've ever facilitated or participated in a book discussion that touched on emotional topics, you've already engaged in the kind of bibliotherapy-like work that libraries are actually built to offer: connecting readers to relevant material and offering an informal venue to talk about it. This is what the phrase *accidental bibliotherapist* is meant to convey—that librarians already do aspects of this work.

The goal here is not to transform yourself from an accidental bibliotherapist into a professional one, but rather into an *intentional bibliotherapy-informed librarian*. We hope to help librarians be more intentional about the ways they facilitate therapeutic reading, and also intentional about setting boundaries between library practice and mental health therapy. Being an intentional bibliotherapy-informed librarian means preparing and setting clear expectations for the kinds of discussions around therapeutic reading that you can facilitate in your library, rather than wandering (or leaping) into a therapeutic role haphazardly and perhaps biting off more than you can chew. The role of an intentional bibliotherapy-informed librarian is to connect patrons to resources rather than to oversee treatment—and this includes referring someone to mental health counseling when appropriate rather than allowing the library to take its place. So if you're wary of becoming an emotional resource for patrons in a way that leaves you feeling drained or risks letting them get hurt, rest assured that we will not ask you to take on that role, and we will provide some strategies to help you keep discussions from becoming overwhelming for you or your participants. The box of tissues in your office should still be primarily for allergy sufferers!

Instead of asking librarians to take on mental health work that they are not necessarily qualified or eager for, we focus on the aspects of bibliotherapy that can be implemented in libraries based on the skills that librarians already have. Remember, you have the background, training, and empathy not only to recommend and discuss books, but also to do it effectively, in multiple ways, for diverse audiences, drawing upon on your familiarity with your audiences and collections. You already possess the expertise to interact with your users and recommend them the next book to read. You have selected, acquired, and organized library materials. You have not only provided information about books but also shared your enthusiasm related to reading. You have hosted events, perhaps even book clubs, and you may be a social media whiz too. Your task now is to leverage those skills more fully to connect your patrons with meaningful reading material.

How Bibliotherapy Works

Read one book or article about bibliotherapy and it will definitely inspire you to try your hand at it. Read several books and articles, and you will probably get confused and start second-guessing yourself. It doesn't mean you should ditch the idea!

If it helps to calm your nerves, keep in mind that the success of a bibliotherapy-inspired program in your library doesn't hinge on any single factor. For example, if you are concerned about selection, keep in mind that the text itself, in isolation, isn't therapeutic. The change takes place in the reader as they respond to the text—that is, through the bibliotherapeutic process, which is ultimately up to the reader, though a librarian can facilitate it. This process is often described in scholarship as consisting of several steps. Below are two models that have been proposed.

The Classic: A Three-Step Model of Bibliotherapy

Bibliotherapy in both clinical and community settings has been theorized as a three-stage process: (1) identification, including projection and introjection, (2) catharsis, and (3) insight (figure 1.1).[1]

FIGURE 1.1

The classic three-step model of bibliotherapy

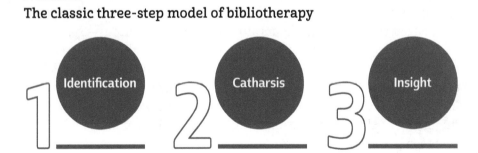

First, the reader finds something in the text that engages them: something that catches their attention, or some associations with a character or situation. Identification is an empathic response. Some texts are more relatable than others, but it largely depends on the target audience and, to a smaller extent, on your intuition—how you select a text that speaks to your readers. For example, when tackling the challenge of launching a three-month reading club called Summer Tales for college students in the beginning of the COVID-19 pandemic in 2020, we picked stories approachable to read and rich to talk about. F. Scott Fitzgerald's "Sleeping and Waking" served as a great first story in many settings; anyone who had ever had trouble sleeping or late-night anxiety can relate. "How to Talk to Girls at Parties" by Neil Gaiman was more specific to this age group or anyone who has ever tried to act cool when secretly scared and confused. These stories have proven great choices for their ability to reward readers at any level of sophistication or engagement, from casual to intense. Students who wanted a seminar- or book club–style discussion could enjoy one, while those who simply wanted to read along and listen to the thoughts of their peers could do so without feeling like eavesdroppers. Students really connected with the stories: in the live discussions as well as in their long, thoughtful posts, many participants related their own personal experiences to the situations depicted in the stories.

In the second stage, the emotional response to the text is followed by catharsis, when the reader, who identified with feelings and thoughts they found relevant in the text, may address their own feelings and thoughts they recalled while reading. These emotions might be rather intense as the reader realizes the ways they share experiences with a fictional character or story, potentially even bringing back memories of unsettled situations, but with the potential of a different responses. Selection of reading materials is key here as well, and it should be based on the target audience and the current environment.

Insight, the final stage, occurs after the above realizations—that is, the reader can identify with the character and can relate to the situation in the text. However, rather than approaching the problem only emotionally, the reader shifts their mindset to a more intellectual level. As they start reflecting on their personal feelings and circumstances, they begin to understand the reasons behind their actions and behaviors. They perhaps might be able to express themselves creatively through writing or arts. Insight into others, the recognition of others beyond their own self, may expand their perspective and cast their own concerns in a new light.

The Complex: Four Steps of Bibliotherapy

Arleen Hynes and Mary Hynes-Berry have elaborated the above process into a more complex model (figure 1.2).[2] In step 1, recognition, readers recognize their understanding of a character or experience either spontaneously or as a response to others' comments in a group discussion. They can recognize unacknowledged feelings or patterns of response sometimes immediately, sometimes gradually. Recognition is an individualized process, and readers in a group may need some time to get accustomed to feeling safe and sharing observations. As they are deeply touched by this experience of recognition, catharsis ("a profound experience of recognition," in Hynes and Hynes-Berry's terminology[3]) might take place at this stage.

FIGURE 1.2

A four-step model of bibliotherapy

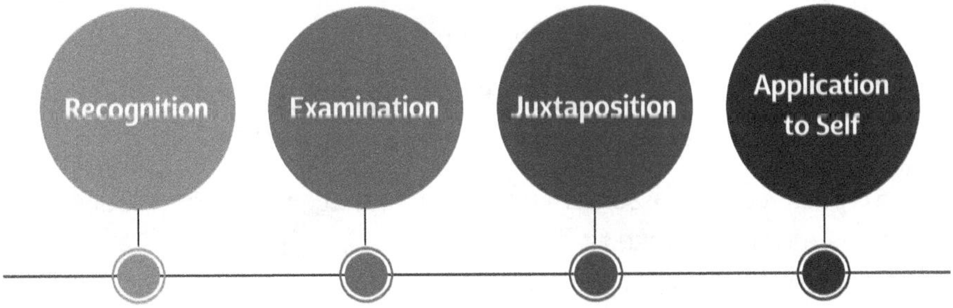

The second step intensifies the first. The reader examines the problems recognized and continues to ask and answer questions related to them: who, what, when, where, why, how, and how much. In a group, participants might be able to examine their responses with the help of a skillful facilitator, who can also guide them as to which of the potential issues they might focus on productively.

Examination leads to step 3, called juxtaposition: putting impressions of the same object side by side. Having examined more deeply the issues raised by the readings, the readers return to consider their first responses. They compare their original feelings and ideas to the new ones brought to light during the examination phase, resulting in several possible responses.

A literary work may contain elements that lead to revelations, such as challenging readers' incorrect or self-limiting assumptions. Fictitious characters can serve as role models for new behavior, or even negative role models—a chance for readers to recognize aspects of themselves or their own behavior that they might want to change.

Step 4 is the application of what has been discovered to the self. Evaluating feelings and ideas at a new level of recognition and examination, the reader looks inward to examine how their attitudes and behaviors can be affected by the new viewpoints provided by the reading. Integrating the insights gained through the process leads to self-awareness in this last stage, the reader moves on to more active behaviors. As Hynes and Hynes-Berry put it, "Although it acts as a reference point for discussion, the literature nonetheless continues to act as a catalyst rather than as the direct focus of self-application."[4]

THE FOUR-STEP MODEL
OF BIBLIOTHERAPY EXPLAINED

Step 1: Recognition: something in the text that engages the reader
- Unacknowledged feelings resurface.
- Patterns of responses are recognized.
- Catharsis might occur.

Step 2: Examination: an intensification of step 1

Step 3: Juxtaposition: first response and additional impressions sit side by side
- Literature corrects discrepancies.
- Literature offers potential role models.
- Literature depicts alternatives.

Step 4: Application to self
- Evaluation: New levels of recognition and examination are reached.
- Self-awareness in the final stage helps move to more creative behaviors.

Adapted from Arleen McCarty Hynes and Mary Hynes-Berry, *Bibliotherapy—the Interactive Process: A Handbook* (Boulder, CO: Westview, 1986), 44–54.

FIGURE 1.3

Comparison of the two models of bibliotherapy

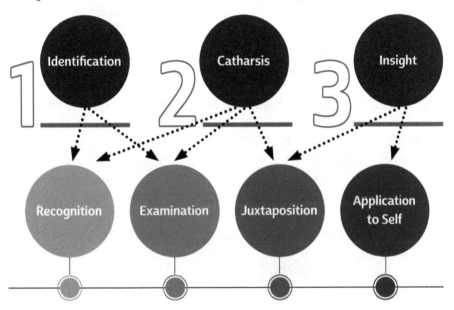

Which model works best for my program?

Now, you might wonder, which model is better? Which should you use? What works best in libraries? Our answer is that both of these models are really just tools for understanding the interactions between readers and texts—there's not a significant practical difference between programs based on one model or the other. The differences between them might be interesting for researchers, but the similarities are what matter most for practitioners, especially accidental bibliotherapists!

The key insights here are that bibliotherapy is a process rather than a single event and that there's no single model for what that process "should" look like. Your job is to facilitate the reader's progressive engagement with the text rather than trying to fit that engagement into a preconceived version of that process. These stages simply attempt to describe a process that is fundamentally internal and self-directed, the magic that happens between text and reader. If you can aid it by thoughtfully choosing a text and putting it in the hands of a reader who can get something out of it, you've already done the part you can control as well as you can; the rest is up to the reader. Your role is to walk with them through their journey (or as some might say, creative act) to discover new, unexpected connections.

Bibliotherapy: A Working Definition for Librarians

What is the "ultimate" definition of *bibliotherapy*? It consists of inter-pretations, approaches, processes, and disciplinary factors. In this book, *bibliotherapy* simply refers to the use of books from a list created under the guidance of a subject expert to address a therapeutic need or boost wellness in any active or passive way. Think of the library as an intellectual pharmacy, where, as "accidental bibliotherapists," librarians dispense reading material from curated lists based on the library's holdings and create guided reading programs to serve the needs of patrons and community members.

───────────── *In a Nutshell* ─────────────

Although there's no consensus on the definition, methods, and practices of bibliotherapy, the more you understand about the process, the more confident you will become that you are capable of running a program inspired by tried-and-true bibliotherapy practices. Rather than putting you in a role better suited to a professional therapist, this book aims to transform you from an "accidental bibliotherapist" into an intentional bibliotherapy-informed librarian. It will highlight the aspects of therapeutic reading that libraries already facilitate, and it will help you design and implement programs appropriate to your library's setting and your own expertise as a librarian. Ultimately, learning more about bibliotherapy will provide a new perspective on the work you already do, empower you to do that work more intentionally, and enhance your toolkit as a librarian.

─────
NOTES

1. Caroline Shrodes, "Bibliotherapy," *Reading Teacher* 9, no. 1 (1955): 24–29.
2. Arleen McCarty Hynes and Mary Hynes-Berry, *Bibliotherapy—the Interactive Process: A Handbook* (Boulder, CO: Westview Press, 1986).
3. Hynes and Hynes-Berry, *Bibliotherapy*, 47.
4. Hynes and Hynes-Berry, 54.

02 | A Brief History of Bibliotherapy

Catharsis, as we know from Aristotle's *Poetics*, is the processing of emotions through art (from Greek: "purgation" or "purification"). For Aristotle, this was part of the spectator's reaction to tragedy on stage; but the concept has become part of our vocabulary ever since for describing the therapeutic effects of artworks across genres and media. This chapter presents some vignettes from that long history of therapeutic reading from Aristotle to today, reflecting changes in both literary history and the history of mental health. Here we share pearls of wisdom in the form of words from pioneers in the field. We've been inspired by their example, and we hope you will be too.

Treating Mental Illness as Illness: Benjamin Rush

One of the first descriptions of psychiatric disorders and their treatment in American medicine was published by the founding father and physician Benjamin Rush, also famous for his pioneering work on alcohol and addiction. In keeping with his humanitarian approach to mental illness—considering it as an ailment to be treated, rather than a moral failing or sign of divine disfavor—Rush was one of the first American medical authorities to recommend the use of bibliotherapy.

For the amusement and instruction of patients in the hospital, a small library should by all means compose a part of its furniture. The amusing books should consist of travels. They are extremely exhilarating to convalescents, and to persons confined by chronic diseases. The books for conveying knowledge should be upon philosophical, moral and religious subjects.[1]

A Literary Clinic from 1916: Samuel McChord Crothers

The first known use of the word *bibliotherapy* is in an article, not completely free from irony, entitled "A Literary Clinic" and written by Samuel McChord Crothers in *The Atlantic Monthly*.[2] In the article, Crothers relates following up on this sign he found in his church's vestry:

> Bibliopathic Institute. Book Treatment by Competent Specialists. Dr. Bagster meets patients by appointment. Free Clinic 2–4 p.m. Out-patients looked after in their homes by members of the Social Services Department. Young People's Lend-a-Thought Club every Sunday evening at 7:30. Tired

FIGURE 2.1

Benjamin Rush, 1813

Source: David Edwin after Thomas Sully, "Gift of Joseph Delaplaine," Pennsylvania Academy of the Fine Arts, www.pafa.org/museum/collection/item/benjamin-rush-m-d.

FIGURE 2.2

Samuel McChord Crothers, circa 1906

Source: Photo by Boston Purdy, "The Rev. S. M. Crothers, author of 'The Gentle Reader,' etc.," in *Critic*, March 1906, 201, available from Wikimedia Commons, commons.wikimedia.org/wiki/File:Portrait_of_Samuel_McChord_Crothers.jpg.

Business Men in classes. Tired Business Men's tired wives given individual treatment. Tired mothers who are reading for health may leave their children in the Day Nursery.[3]

The article relates Crothers's conversation with Bagster and offers insight into an early but recognizable version of bibliotherapy. According to Bagster's selection policies, a book he considers a literary prescription should always contain:

1. A basis, or chief ingredient intended to cure.
2. An adjuvant, to assist the action and make it cure more quickly.
3. A corrective, to prevent or lessen any undesirable effect.
4. A vehicle, or excipient, to make it suitable for administration and pleasant to the patient.[4]

Bagster's pharmaceutical metaphor—the reading as a cocktail of treatments, wrapped in a sugarcoating of literary pleasure—lays the foundation for bibliotherapy for more than a century to come. As he beautifully puts it, "Certain books are stimulants. They do not so much furnish us with thoughts as set us thinking. They awaken faculties which we had allowed to be dormant. After reading them we actually feel differently and frequently we act differently. The book is a spiritual event."[5]

READER, CHALLENGE YOURSELF

For content, Crothers recommends that readers challenge themselves:

> "You must read more novels. Not pleasant stories that make you forget yourself. They must be searching, drastic, stinging, relentless novels, without any alleviations of humor or any sympathy with human weakness, designed to make you miserable. They will show you up."

Samuel McChord Crothers, "A Literary Clinic," *Atlantic Monthly*, September 1916, 296.

In his view, therapeutic reading is not a soothing painkiller but a kind of physical therapy of the spirit, provoking thought and pushing capacities. Our own approach, and contemporary practice, is not so uncompromising when it comes to "sympathy for human weakness" and "humor"—laughter, after all, is the best medicine! But Crothers's prescription reminds us that "therapeutic" reading does not necessarily mean easy answers; instead, it allows participants to explore difficult questions more deeply and to experience the full range of difficult emotions, through the mediation of a good book.

Psychological Dietetics by Hospital Librarians: Gordon Kamman

One of the earliest supporters and practitioners of bibliotherapy was the physician Gordon Kamman, who advocated for professional hospital librarians to take up this role, as they would realize what might be contraindicated to one patient or outright harmful to the next one. He discouraged allowing untrained volunteers, nurses, physiotherapists, or anyone else to dispense reading material to patients:

"This is as unscientific as it would be to allow the occupational therapist to do medical social service work, or to ask the physiotherapist to supervise the diet of a patient suffering from renal insufficiency." [6]

Kamman referred to bibliotherapy as "a form of psychological dietetics which requires close cooperation between physicians and bibliotherapists," the latter ideally a hospital librarian.

Reading may be ordered either for rehabilitational or for recreational purposes. It provides a sedative for mental

FIGURE 2.3
Gordon Kamman, 1943

Source: Courtesy of the National Library of Medicine.

excitement and tonic for depression. One may lose one's self in a good book as one does in sleep. Healing progresses more rapidly when the individual's mind is off himself. Through books the isolated individual may roam the world. This provides mental diversion and gives less time about temperature, pulse, outcome of illness, and its possible residual handicap. Furthermore, reading replaces gossip.[7]

(We like to think that reading and gossip can coexist!)

Early Research on Bibliotherapy: William Menninger

A pioneer physician advocating the use of books in treating mental illness, William Menninger not only incorporated books into his treatment plans but also conducted one of the very first research projects on prescribing reading material as a therapeutic measure in hospitalized patients. In a lecture he gave to the American Psychiatric Association on May 14, 1937, in Pittsburgh, Pennsylvania, he presented his results based on the data he collected from eighteen outstanding hospitals.[8] He found a general approval of bibliotherapy, although he pointed out the "indifference of execution as a treatment method" and the lack of efforts to evaluate the results.[9] His investigations on book selection and book prescription revealed five hospitals without therapeutic reading programs at all. In seven hospitals, everything was left to the librarian, while in one hospital the physician gave occasional suggestions to the librarian. Menninger found only three places where a physician gave specific reading recommendations. The librarian in all instances was directly responsible

FIGURE 2.4

William Menninger, circa 1943

Source: United States Army, "Will Menninger in His Official U.S. Army Brigadier General Portrait circa 1943," available from https://commons. wikimedia.org/wiki/File:William_Claire _Menninger.jpg.

for the book selection and prescription as well as for the direction of the program and its evaluation.

Menninger identified three factors as the basis for prescribing a book: the patient's current therapeutic needs, the patient's background, and the actual symptoms. Therapeutic needs might mean providing help, gaining insight, or reading for recreational purposes. A key for Menninger was background—that is, the patient's reading ability, interests, gender, and occupation. Menninger said the prescription should be based not strictly on diagnostics or personality, but "rather on the individual's present psychological status, namely, his emotional state, the amount of his withdrawal from reality, and his capacity at the moment to read and to gain something from what he reads."[10]

Throughout the process of prescription, to be performed by the librarian, responsibilities included purchasing, maintaining, and distributing books. The librarian (always a "she" in his text) was to have a "personal acquaintance" with the books and should interview each patient and collect their impressions gained from the reading followed by a written report on the interview submitted to the physician. Menninger concluded that there was "a wide variety of therapeutic needs, types of personalities, and limitless variety of reading materials" and "the reading [was] only a small part in a total program of therapy," recommending bibliotherapy as an adjuvant rather than primary form of treatment.[11] Menninger was one of the first to advocate a team approach, pointing out that no single person is well versed in all fields (literature, psychology, therapy) to assume full responsibility in a hospital bibliotherapy program.[12]

The Science of Bibliotherapy: Alice Bryan

In a seminal 1939 article, the psychologist Alice Bryan wondered if there could be a "science" of bibliotherapy and decided, based on research into the relationship between emotional states and physical conditions, that the answer was yes.[13] Her article drew on then new studies in the journal *Psychosomatic Medicine*, confirming connections between emotional issues and ailments such as gastrointestinal and cardiovascular diseases, asthma, diabetes, skin diseases, and accidents.[14] (If this sounds farfetched, think about the way that stress compounds physical conditions like heartburn, tension, skin issues, and so on.) Bryan was one of the first modern writers to encourage cooperation between physicians and librarians to help address both psychological and physical complaints.

> The assumption that stimulation received through reading may affect an individual's emotions, attitudes and subsequent behavior is as old as the art of living itself. That the effect of reading may be qualitatively good or bad, depending upon the type of material read and the emotional and intellectual maturity of the reader, has likewise been accepted almost as a truism. [. . .]
>
> Educators seem agreed that if people find such materials amusing or entertaining, they should not only be permitted but encouraged to read them as a wholesome way of utilizing leisure time. Thus, to the educational function of reading may be added the recreational. Still another function of reading may theoretically be differentiated from these. To the extent that the printed word may induce reactions beneficial to the individual's physical or mental health, reading may be said to have therapeutic value.[15]

A Pioneer Black Woman in the Segregated South: Sadie Peterson Delaney

While physicians and psychologists were laying the theoretical foundations for this "science of bibliotherapy," librarians played a crucial role in its development as well—both as theorists and as practitioners. The librarian Sadie Delaney, a Black woman working at a VA hospital in segregated Alabama, implemented guided therapeutic reading programs for her veteran patrons and published on her work contemporaneously with Menninger and Bryan. Delaney approached

FIGURE 2.5

Sadie P. Delaney, 1915

Source: The *Quill*, a parish publication of the AME Zion Church, Poughkeepsie, New York, Dutchess County Historical Society, Walter Patrice Collection.

bibliotherapy not as a single kind of clinical interaction, but as a framework to highlight and promote the wide array of services and programs her library offered and their potential therapeutic benefits. In Delaney's own words:

> Books[,] like medicine, have a definite effect on the physical, mental and moral welfare of those who are unfortunately handicapped by illness. The library then has become a laboratory and the workshop for those interested in the improvement and development of the whole individual. Here, minds long imprisoned in lethargy are awakened. This has been evident at the hospital library of the Veterans' Administration Facility, Tuskegee, Alabama[,] for 14 years.[16]

ASK THE EXPERT

DAVID TATE
Who Was Sadie Peterson Delaney?

David Tate is the author of "Offprinting Bibliotherapy: Sadie P. Delaney's Interventions in Media Infrastructures" in the fall 2022 issue of *Book History*.

Sadie Peterson Delaney (1889–1958) was a librarian, born in Poughkeepsie, New York, and trained in New York City at the New York Public Library. She spent her career caring for Black veterans at the Tuskegee Medical Center in Alabama from the 1920s until her death. Famous during her lifetime and now as a highly successful practitioner of bibliotherapy, Delaney in fact provided an enormous and wide-ranging amount of book-centered and book-adjacent activities for the patients in her charge. Prescribed reading was just one part of this larger project, which included sessions on bookbinding, translating, library curating, and even stamp collecting. Even so, Delaney emphasized bibliotherapy in marketing her library programs, circulating articles—often written by other people—about her library activities across the United States and the world to fundraise for and publicize her mission in Tuskegee. It could be argued that for this founder, "bibliotherapy" as a single, clinical model for therapeutic reading did not actually exist; rather, it stood in for a diverse array of undertakings based in the hospital library that Delaney was originally tasked to build. In this way, Delaney, a Black woman working with Black veterans in the segregated South, was able to develop an immensely successful educational enterprise, using bibliotherapy not as a clinical practice grafted onto a library setting but as a way of reframing and strategically marketing elements of her library's core mission—the wide range of programs she deemed beneficial for the patients to whom she devoted her life.

Delaney tried to join the Alabama Library Association, which did not allow Black people to become members at the time. She was eventually invited to join, but the incoming president discontinued her membership in 1951. She received an honorary doctorate from Atlanta University in 1950. In her acceptance speech, she said:

> Tonight I know more than I shall be able to express, if I live to be 100, of the contentment one gains through service to humanity. If I have contributed anything at all, it has been in exploring new fields in hospital library service by using empirical methods until perfection could be attained. . . . I have tried to share my discoveries with other libraries.[17]

The "Accidental Bibliotherapist" and a Critical History of Bibliotherapy: Liz Brewster

Acknowledging the current role of librarians as "accidental bibliotherapists" couldn't have happened without the extensive research conducted by Liz Brewster, currently a medical educator in the mental health field in the United Kingdom. Brewster coined the phrase in 2009, using it in the title of an article published in *Australasian Public Libraries and Information Services*. Ever since, the concept has been empowering librarians without formal training or a license in therapy to assist patrons and connect them with the right book at the right time, while also legitimizing bibliotherapy-inspired programs in libraries to promote general well-being.[18]

Further Reading: Bibliotherapy and Libraries Today

If you wish to read more on the history of bibliotherapy, pick up a copy of *Bibliotherapy*, a recent landmark contribution to the field edited by Sarah McNichol and the above-mentioned Liz Brewster.[19] The book provides a comprehensive view of the field for both scholars and practitioners, including librarians, presenting case studies from across the world.

One of Brewster's own contributions to the volume, "Bibliotherapy: A Critical History," traces the field's emergence and development over the course of the twentieth century and into the twenty-first. Moreover, she shows how the primary venues for bibliotherapy have shifted over the last few decades from hospital and clinical settings to libraries. The whole book is well worth reading, but that conclusion alone should reassure librarians that they can indeed implement bibliotherapeutic ideas and practices: libraries have had a place in bibliotherapy from the field's very beginning, and today that place is at the head of the table.

In a Nutshell

This brief history of bibliotherapy is meant to suggest that librarians are not interlopers in bibliotherapy, but rather have been involved in the field from the beginning. Stocking your intellectual pharmacy with remedies that can help patrons when needed is part of everyday collection development, while finding out about that pressing need falls under the carefully executed reference interview. While librarians do not pledge the famous Hippocratic oath, they nevertheless approach their patrons with attention and care that the creators of bibliotherapy described above envisioned for practitioners. With a proper recognition of the difference between clinical mental health practice and guided reading, you can feel empowered and encouraged by bibliotherapy's longstanding ties to library practice, knowing that you can, in fact, use your expertise to guide patrons through meaningful interactions with books and fellow readers.

NOTES

1. Benjamin Rush, *Sixteen Introductory Lectures to Courses of Lectures upon the Institutes and Practice of Medicine, with a Syllabus of the Latter. to which are Added, Two Lectures upon the Pleasures of the Senses and of the Mind, with an Inquiry into their Proximate Cause: Delivered in the University of Pennsylvania* (Philadelphia: Bradford and Innskeep, 1811), 192.
2. Samuel McChord Crothers, "A Literary Clinic," *Atlantic Monthly*, September 1916, 291–301, esp. 295.
3. Crothers, "Literary Clinic," 291.
4. Crothers, 293.
5. Crothers, 293.
6. Gordon Kamman, "The Role of Bibliotherapy in Care of the Patient," *Bulletin of the American College of Surgeons* 24 (1939): 183–84.
7. Kamman, "Role of Bibliotherapy," 183.
8. William Menninger, "Bibliotherapy," *Bulletin of the Menninger Clinic* 1, no. 8 (1937): 263–74.
9. Menninger, "Bibliotherapy," 266.
10. Menninger, 267.
11. Menninger, 269.
12. See Menninger, 267–68.
13. Alice I. Bryan, "Can There Be a Science of Bibliotherapy?," *Library Journal* 64, no. 18 (1939): 773–76.
14. Bryan, "Can There Be a Science?," 774.
15. Bryan, 773.
16. Sadie Peterson Delaney, "The Place of Bibliotherapy in a Hospital," *Opportunity Journal* 16, no. 2 (1938): 53.
17. Quoted in Betty K. Gubert, "Sadie Peterson Delaney: Pioneer Bibliotherapist," *American Libraries* 24, no. 2 (1993): 129.

18. Liz Brewster, "Reader Development and Mental Wellbeing: The Accidental Bibliotherapist," *Australasian Public Libraries and Information Services* 22, no. 1 (2009):13–16, https://doi.org/10.3316/ielapa.639346 863805647.

19. See Sarah McNicol and Liz Brewster, *Bibliotherapy* (London: Facet, 2018).

PART II

Turning Inward

03 | Bibliotherapy in Your Library

Have we lit a fire under you yet? We'd be willing to bet you already have a program idea or maybe even a full concept! This chapter outlines a few basic steps to get started (some might even be helpful for general planning), focusing on key elements involved in conceptualizing, designing, and creating library-based bibliotherapy programs. We are fully aware that it would be impossible to list all the necessary components from A to Z and that each library has its own bottlenecks. Nonetheless, we advocate for careful planning. Consider common factors such as accommodation, amenities, availability, budget, collection, community demographics, human resources, and your library's mission. The steps in this chapter can easily be expanded, cut, and tailored to your own setting.

Set Your Vision

If you have reached the point where you'd like to start your own program, you already have a general idea of what you'd like to do and how bibliotherapy can add value. Think of your first idea as a seed of a plant, full of potential, depending on you nurturing it. First, research how to germinate the tiny seed—prepping the soil, planting the seed, and tending it as it grows without seeing the flower or fruit for a long period. As you develop your full program and bring this seed to full flower (even through periods of rough weather), you will probably stick with your original, unifying theme, which mirrors your interests, values, and principles.

AT A GLANCE

- Set Your Vision
- Follow the $$$
- Work with What You Have
- Know Thy Users
- Get Buy-In (aka Try Participatory Design)
- Get Approved
- Time Your Launch
- Get Feedback
- Create Synergies

You already have a portfolio of your practice, perhaps with an official vision statement that reflects who you are and how you serve your patrons. You may want to lean into it and start right there first. As with research or reading, we recommend picking something you're passionate about. Whether you've chosen bibliotherapy as a tool or, as it often happens in libraries, you've been chosen to explore the potential of bibliotherapy-inspired programming to attract and engage patrons, conceptualizing your program is the proverbial first step in your journey.

Your vested interest is key to set your vision. You already know your target population, the often limited capacity of your library with its constraints, the local management approaches, and your own appetite for difficulty and risk. Expect your concept to evolve further and adjust your plan accordingly, until you can enjoy the full blossom and the fruit of the seed you planted without upsetting the applecart.

TABLE 3.1

Program Template

With so many questions to ask and decisions to make ahead of time, this chart might help design a bibliotherapy program in your library.

	DECISION POINTS	NOTES
TIME		
Length of program	Semester long? All summer? Shorter duration?	Developing trust in group takes time Watch out for major holidays
Frequency	Once a week? Once a month?	Low frequency: may lose participation High frequency: may present scheduling problems
Length of session	60 minutes? 90 minutes? Overtime?	Attention spans vary (e.g., age of target audience)
Schedule	Weekday or weekend? Morning, midday, evening?	Convenience for participants Availability of space Watch out for major holidays and other programs

	DECISION POINTS	NOTES
DELIVERY		
Venue	Onsite or remote? In the library or other physical location?	Remote: online access, software
		Onsite: availability of space
AUDIENCE		
	Defined by age group? Special topic? Local flavor/ community interests?	Suggested discussion group sizes: 4–8 online, 10–12 in person
READING MATERIAL		
Theme and topic	Theme and reading material to select?	Select early
	Length? Accessibility of text (in collection/free online)?	Consider diversity and inclusion
	Possible challenges?	Go with comfort level of discussion moderator(s)
Discussion potential	Talking points or questions? Discussion sheets or ad lib?	Adjust to topic and audience
MODERATOR/ SPEAKER		
Choice	Moderator(s): librarian or staff member?	Not all books/topics are preferred by the same person
	Previous or new?	Have backup (external moderators work too)
Guest	Guest speaker/author: local or national name?	Schedule early!
	Funding: by the library or cofunded?	Online format saves money; big-name authors can be expensive

Follow the $$$

Breaking down the larger budget into portions to be used for various programs can sometimes be quite a challenge for the library director. Understanding where your library stands in the midst of budget cuts, layoffs, and competing or even opposing priorities is part of the big-picture approach that can be hard to see but lays a foundation for success. Make sure your program is realistic for your library's capacities: for instance, if a program claims an unreasonably large percentage of a decreasing budget, it is likely destined for the chopping block no matter how brilliant its ideas.

A safe start to consider is piggybacking on an existing or well-established program, such as summer reading for public and school libraries. Starting small before you get your ducks in a row is also a good and inexpensive method to test the waters: for example, a few sessions discussing short stories might be a good way to pilot a longer and more resource-intensive yearlong book club, gauging and demonstrating community interest before committing to a big initiative. The experience gained with this initial setup can also serve as guidelines for planning and marketing strategies in the long run.

Work with What You Have

In general, it's easier to build on available assets in terms of human resources. Thrown into the deep end to run projects—including challenging ones during the pandemic—we became devoted fans of working with what we already have at hand. Instead of lofty goals, which often come with expensive, hard-to-justify talent acquisitions, it's safer to start a new program by tapping into available skills for the program. Do you have an avid reader on staff? A fan of graphic novels? A mystery buff? A talented artist? A self-made graphic designer? A social media butterfly? Your colleagues may be eager to have their unique skillsets recognized and applied, revealing talents that had only been hinted at previously—a challenge can be invigorating.

For example, for an audience of college students, perhaps you already have a student worker or can recruit a volunteer closer in age to your target group who can communicate with them in different ways than a librarian can. If your target audience consists of or includes non-native speakers, perhaps reach out to a facilitator or even a participant of the ESL conversation group. A reading group in another language (such as Spanish) will of course require a bilingual staff member with native or near-native proficiency. Not all staff capabilities are as mandatory as that, of course, but if you lack the personnel knowledge, skills, and abilities for your desired program, you may want to consider recalibrating your goals.

Know Thy Users

Identifying the audience for a program and designing it with their needs and wants in mind is crucial. Understanding the demographics of your participants, whether they are already library users or not, is even more relevant for bibliotherapy-inspired projects with their great potential in engaging more diverse audiences. You never know who will get suddenly interested in a new program (think of underserved segments of the community) and become a new library user via joining your program, or who might be drawn in by recreational reading and then discover the library as a useful place to fulfill their information needs. If you build and promote your program in the right way, they will come. This is also the point at which you might start thinking about your program's name, logo, promotional text, and other marketing elements.

Getting familiar with library users and matching your program to them starts with just looking around your library. For example, if your library is a place where retirees come over from the neighborhood retirement communities or the senior center every Friday, a program with topics of interest targeting this age group should also incorporate special formats such as large print or audio—multiple formats are ideal for users with sensory impairments, common among seniors but potentially a concern for other users as well. At the other end of the age spectrum, high school or teenage users may be interested in different topics that relate more to their own life experiences and might need more prodding or hand-holding to stay on task.

Get Buy-In (aka Try Participatory Design)

Once you have an idea of your own resources and your participants' needs, as well as a clear vision of what you're planning to do, you can start inviting others to contribute. By that, we mean casting a wide net to find out about participant expectations and to ensure that your outcomes meet their needs. Actively involving all stakeholders in the design process works well in libraries.

RUTGERS STUDENTS INSPIRE BIBLIOTHERAPY-FOCUSED PROGRAM

The inspiration for the very first iteration of an on-campus biblio-therapy-focused program in a science library at Rutgers began with a 2018 landscape architecture course project aiming to hypo-thetically redesign our library. Based on their research, onsite observations, interviews, and other techniques, the forty-four university students involved in the program made practical recom-mendations for more engagement, more programming, and more fun reading in the library. We saw an opening for a guided reading program that spoke to students' experiences and concerns, and the Books We Read project (go.rutgers.edu/booksweread) was born, enfolding onsite programs, one-shot events, and semes-ter-long engagement alike. The initiative not only survived the pandemic but also turned into a flagship program of the entire library system, providing countless outreach and collaboration opportunities in the online-only environment.

As librarians excel at building relationships with users, we should rec-ognize the value of informal chitchats and anecdotal evidence alongside more formal information gathering. Sometimes that one user who always stops by the reference desk and has a question or the one who starts a con-versation every time they check out books at circulation might eventually act as the spokesperson for a much larger group.

Participatory design is especially useful in bibliotherapy-inspired pro-grams, which aim to help participants discuss topics and process issues of concern—different themes are going to be relevant to different users, and the best way to know what *your* users or community members are looking for is to ask them! You'll want to gather this information in a respectful and noninvasive way, of course, especially if dealing with sensitive subjects. An open-ended survey about what kinds of topics participants might want to discuss or see reflected in the readings—or even those casual conversations with current users—can help make sure you're responding to community interest and not flying blind. In addition to ensuring that your program is relevant for users, even a little bit of participatory design fosters buy-in among participants by demonstrating that you're listening to them. Don't hesitate to let participants know when you've taken their advice or if certain features of the program were designed in response to survey results—they'll appreciate that their input matters.

Get Approved

With a specific vision, a realistic budget, and relevant content, hopefully your project will be approved, especially if you've included some of the decision makers and ensured their buy-in during the early phases. Again, lobbying for a project depends largely on local factors and where the library stands in its growth. Even the best-designed projects can slip on an overlooked detail or a single disgruntled stakeholder.

At the risk of stating the obvious: to put together a winning project proposal, you will probably need someone with excellent writing skills, in addition to picking the brains of your trusted friends or simply counting on a second pair of eyes to proofread. While some people might seem to write well effortlessly, it's a learned skill, and a valuable one for you or a team member to have—or to learn! The goal is to deliver a clean copy of your project proposal, written in language that your prospective readers and decision makers will understand readily. A few images, charts, or tables are fine, as long as they are justifiable—that is, they add value to the entire proposal and don't simply illustrate it.

Time Your Launch

Timing when to launch your project may be tricky, but you can rely on what you have found out from your stakeholders. Librarians already know how futile it is to schedule an event around major holidays or, in an academic institution, during the start-of-semester crunch. All our marketing efforts would go to waste trying to beat Halloween or the Super Bowl!

A longer program seems to be more successful if it starts with a bang. It's a little bit more work to prepare for one big event in addition to starting a program that will last for several months, but this is the time when you can start thinking about creating synergies.

Get Feedback

Participants, users, guests, and visitors love to share their sentiments whether, as personal comments on a social media post, filling out surveys (which works better when there's a chance to win a prize), or even dropping an anonymous suggestion into a well-positioned box in the library. Anonymous might be the operational word for many bibliotherapy-related views and criticism. Feedback is important for evaluating the actual program as well as the marketing. Soliciting feedback about a program or service might bring in ideas to improve, but whether or not the specific suggestions are helpful will always allow you to better understand your audience. These practices go hand in hand: forging relationships with your audience lays the groundwork for soliciting feedback that forms a key part of your assessment, and assessing your outreach efforts allows you to focus on what worked and fix what didn't for your next program launch.

Create Synergies

A critical element in developing bibliotherapy-related programs is building on synergies between different events and library programs. Some of these can be accomplished intentionally and proactively, while others will happen as happy accidents.

You might be lucky enough to already work in an environment that fosters synergies. If you are not, running a bibliotherapy-inspired program is a great opportunity to prove the advantages of such an approach. Synergies combine mutually advantageous components, resources, or efforts—or even entire operations—in related actions. For example, repurposing materials across different programs, creating templates to simplify your work, and collaborating with community partners all can help your efforts go further and create effects that are greater than the sum of their parts. It pays to be attentive to those synergies as you go along. And save your work: these early big-picture thoughts about the design of your program, for instance, might be helpful to consult when deciding how to market the program to potential audiences or when assessing how well the program has delivered on its goals.

In a Nutshell

There is no single, foolproof method to create a successful program. This chapter suggests a step-by-step process to get you started on your own bibliotherapy-inspired program in your library. The phases translate easily to marketing strategies necessary to promote bibliotherapy initiatives across libraries and platforms. You are a librarian, trained and skilled at collecting and organizing information, cataloging resources, creating a skills inventory, and putting everything together with your target audiences in mind. Starting small and experimenting—"failing again, and failing better," to rephrase the great writer Samuel Beckett—is the best way to figure out what works best for your library, program, and community.

04 | Passive and Active Programming

Feel like giving it a try? You are at the right place now, literally and figuratively! Whether you know it or not, you have been doing so many related activities that it won't add too much to your workload to look at your practice from a fresh perspective and reap the benefits of infusing your programs with bibliotherapy. Instead, the new angle might just be the gentle nudge you need to get energized and review how patrons can be served better. This chapter discusses the advantages and disadvantages of different modalities of bibliotherapy programs, including "passive" resources such as LibGuides, social media, or blogs. It will help you explore how your current practice compares to what you could be doing. A few examples of successful programs are provided to use as a model to start thinking about designing your own.

The Many Ways to Offer Bibliotherapy in the Library

Bibliotherapy-inspired programs and projects come in all shapes and sizes. Requiring different strategies, time frame, and financial investment, programming initiatives can be divided into passive (such as reading lists, exhibits, LibGuides, and social media posts) and active (such as readers' advisory, small-group discussion, and big events). Building on this classification, you may want to explore the various program modalities and our examples, which illustrate how each might be implemented.

AT A GLANCE

- The Many Ways to Offer Bibliotherapy in the Library
- Passive Programming
- Reading Lists and Book Recommendations
- Book Displays in the Library
- Blogs and Social Media
- Active Programming
- Readers' Advisory
- Group Discussions
- Public Events

It's beyond the scope of this book to elaborate on all possible modalities. However, active and passive programs combined have the chance to create more than the sum of their parts, as they will complement and strengthen each other. Even if you are not yet ready to start a full program, we advocate for considering adding a few elements of bibliotherapy into your current practice. Once comfortable and hooked, you can start experimenting on a smaller scale until you find the best ways to start your own major program.

Passive Programming

Passive modalities are, simply put, aspects of your programming that (once set up) require minimal labor to maintain—they continue working for you on their own. Aside from this obvious advantage, passive modalities also tend to allow patrons to engage at their own time and pace, on their own terms, no scheduled appointments or commitments. The classic here is the book display, but passive modalities might include online reading lists, anthologies, LibGuides, and other supplementary material, all of which can be developed and updated during slower times during work hours and will complement endeavors requiring more active, ongoing staff commitment.

Online modalities in particular deserve special attention: while a certain level of maintenance is just as necessary for online resources as for physical ones (to avoid outdated content, broken links, and so on), web pages can "greet" visitors, introduce your program, offer resources, and more. Library collections and exhibits set up for virtual browsing will not only facilitate discovery, but also may function as visual reminders of the wealth and depth of resources and services in your library, inviting and inspiring for new and timid readers. Related blog posts and complementary social media teasers also serve as promotional materials for marketing your program, adding to the synergies you want to practice habitually.

SAMPLE PASSIVE-RECEPTIVE MODALITIES

- Blogs and social media posts by program leaders and participants
- Book recommendations
- Book displays in the library
- Collections for virtual browsing to facilitate discovery
- Collections specialized in a topic or discipline
- Invited blog posts on a topic
- LibGuides and other supplementary material
- Reading lists, including bibliotherapists' lists
- Thematic anthologies

Reading Lists and Book Recommendations

Reading lists and book recommendations are well-established practices in the library. Bibliotherapeutic lists have been published for decades in print as lists of titles with bibliographic records or annotated with content. The difference is one of focus: a bibliotherapy list is centered around a specific reading purpose or outcome, i.e., the reader's emotional engagement with the text. Bibliotherapy lists are less likely than traditional reading lists to be organized by genre, and while they more closely resemble thematic reading lists, there remains a subtle difference in emphasis; bibliotherapy lists are tailored to readers' emotional needs alongside their intellectual ones.

RESOURCES

Book Recommendations

Before creating your own reading list, you may want to explore one or more of the countless online resources for book recommendations to learn the ropes. To each their own, right? From the many print books to choose from, the following titles stand out with their straightforward approach to bibliotherapy. Pick up one of them to find recommendations of books you already have read or always wanted to read! Additionally, you will also learn all the secrets of how to write an enticing book recommendation yourself and will feel inspired to start putting together your own collection.

- *The Novel Cure: From Abandonment to Zestlessness* by Ella Bethroud and Susan Elderkin lists 751 books claiming to cure pretty much any conditions, physical or mental, small or big. In addition to being hilariously funny (without mocking bibliotherapy), the book is a great resource to browse many titles for fun and therapeutic reading recommendations.
- *Bibliotherapy* by Linda Karges-Bone shares forty-eight children's books across six areas of bibliotherapy: attachment and growth; creativity and critical thinking; bullying and building friendships; family matters (dynamics and change); poverty and social justice issues; and childhood challenges. It features activities to develop listening, speaking, reading, and writing skills, some of which might be of value if you consider extending your own program with additional creative modalities.
- *Read Two Books and Let's Talk Next Week: Using Bibliotherapy in Clinical Practice* by Janice Maidman Joshua and Donna DiMenna lists 317 titles primarily geared toward clinical bibliotherapy, many of which can also be used in a library setting. A great benefit of the book is the structure of the individual book recommendations organized around a basic template, an approach we recommend for your own reading lists. Each recommendation consists of three sections: a brief description of the book, audience, and potential therapeutic benefits or insights.

Ella Bethroud and Susan Elderkin, *The Novel Cure: From Abandonment to Zestlessness: 751 Books to Cure What Ails You* (New York: Penguin, 2013).

Dr. Linda Karges-Bone, *Bibliotherapy* (Dayton: Classroom Complete Press, 2015).

Janice Maidman Joshua and Donna DiMenna, *Read Two Books and Let's Talk Next Week: Using Bibliotherapy in Clinical Practice* (New York: J. Wiley, 2000).

Book Displays in the Library

Booklists and recommendations can also serve as the basis for a library exhibit collating available titles by purpose, theme, or target audience. A strategically positioned, well-organized display of a few books organized by one of the above principles can highlight items from the catalog for better visibility. The display can be permanent (such as addiction memoirs by celebrities, with titles refreshed periodically) or related to a single event (such as fiction and nonfiction related to the topic of an upcoming author talk).

Most importantly for the authors of this book coming from an addiction library, we never underestimate the role of taking an active stance against the stigma associated with certain topics and censorship. A simple display in a strategically positioned spot in the library or on the website will send a powerful message without putting the librarian on the spot in a face-to-face interaction and will set the tone for discussions on these topics.

READING SUGGESTION EXCHANGE

One of the more successful parts of our undergraduate summer reading club at Rutgers was actually initiated in response to students' own practices in discussion. So many students were sharing book recommendations in our forum discussions that we decided to create a dedicated thread to meet the demand (and help keep the other threads focused on the reading at hand): the "Reading Suggestion Exchange." The prompt consisted of three simple questions:

1. What have you read that you think more people should read? Why should people read it?
2. If you and someone else have read the same book, compare your impressions (though please keep it civil if you disagree)!
3. Alternatively, if you're looking for something to read, you can describe the sort of book you like and see if anyone has a recommendation!

Participants eagerly responded, often writing long and thoughtful posts about their favorite books and their emotional responses to them. The opportunity for this kind of participation is a real advantage of asynchronous discussions—and a major benefit of paying attention to what your participants seem most passionate about!

Blogs and Social Media

Blog and social media posts also fall in the passive category, although including a CTA (call to action) option can easily make it interactive. Judging by our site metrics, book reviews on single titles or clusters of books grouped together by author, genre, or topic seem to be very popular, followed by promotional posts on social media. Many libraries have already established a "staff picks" section on their website; through thematic collections and thoughtful tagging, you can expand this section into therapeutic reading recommendations where applicable.

In addition to writing posts of your own, you can invite new voices as guest bloggers. Recruit your colleagues and program participants. To engage a guest blogger, try hosting creative writing contests or soliciting perspectives on a single title. Library staff may want to contribute with their own topic choices related to wellness and mental health. A guest blog post can be based on preset questions and published as an interview, providing a treasure trove of resources with very personal, individual virtual collections inspired by the guest's bibliotherapy-focused mindset.

Active Programming

Active bibliotherapy-inspired practices range from one-on-ones to large group settings and anything in between; they can be virtual or in person, synchronous or asynchronous. Each modality has its own advantages and disadvantages and should be chosen to meet user needs and expectations. These programs tend to require a lot more attention and time, and also vary according to the comfort level of both the librarian and the participants.

Again, you can get started with what you have already been doing and enjoy. Do you like to advise library patrons what to read next? Bibliotherapy-infused readers' advisory can get your foot in the door! Do you get excited picking out books for a book club and running discussions? You may want to look into new wellness-focused topics. Have you been teaching or hosting the local talk show and don't mind the spotlight? You'll love organizing large bibliotherapy-themed events! Whatever your strengths and background, you can hit the ground running on the path toward connecting with your community via bibliotherapy-focused programs.

SAMPLE ACTIVE MODALITIES

- Readers' advisory, one-on-one at the reference desk or virtually
- Small-group discussion online or in the library synchronously
- Asynchronous group discussions online such as on a forum or LMS
- Author talks
- Readouts such as for Banned Books Week
- Program kickoff events
- Program wrap-up events

Readers' Advisory

Providing readers' advisory (RA) services is an art itself, let alone RA with difficult topics. Librarians who already excel in selecting read-alikes and conducting RA interviews can easily turn an RA session into a successful bibliotherapy-focused dialog—with some changes. For a start, even though traditional RA and bibliotherapy-infused RA differ a bit (see table 4.1), you have already mastered the main RA trick to start your journey to a bibliotherapeutic approach: give the reader what they need, but listen to them first! Listen and listen more; listen carefully, seeking to hear what the reader is really trying to say.

The main difference between traditional readers' advisory and biblio-therapy-infused readers' advisory is in the goal, which is not only to suggest texts for fun or self-education but also for therapeutic purposes. The book or text you choose for a bibliotherapy-infused RA should provide insight into the issue or problem that the reader tells you they're grappling with. You want to inspire the reader to read further on their own and identify their own needs. Although any suggestion can be a hit-and-miss affair, we strongly advise that for this type of RA you draw upon your own reading experience rather than traditional RA resources. Your thorough background knowledge of a text and its author is helpful for making an educated guess about whether or not the text will resonate with the reader.

How do you transition your RA into a more reader-centered interaction for bibliotherapeutic purposes? If you work in a library, you have probably established your patron-oriented library services for recreational read-ers—an RA tradition in most public libraries. With small changes in your procedures, your new, collaborative approach can turn your RA work easily into a rich, bibliotherapy-infused practice. As a librarian, you are probably well versed in conducting RA interviews in your library, which lead to an understanding of your patrons' reading habits, likes, and dislikes. Based on what you find out, you routinely suggest literary works from all genres and types of books using traditional RA resources and your collection. You have likely become skilled at sorting out appeal factors and you feel comfortable recommending the next book to read.

Outside the walls of your library, there's a good chance you are also conducting unofficial, peer-to-peer RA—not only face to face with your coworkers, friends, and family, but also on social networking sites, such as Goodreads and LibraryThing. You may even write recaps, book reviews, and recommendations on sites maintained by publishers and book jobbers. This skill can be directly translated into your new RA initiative.

Although the goal to connect the reader with the right book remains, bibliotherapy-infused RA shifts the focus to the reader's inner life and ther-apeutic concerns. Instead of, say, matching the reader's genre preferences, bibliotherapy-centered book recommendations are based on the potential reading experience—how the text resonates with the reader. The only way to get close to what they need is to convert the traditional, one-way RA interview into a two-way reading-experience dialog between you and the reader. You can do that by simply shifting the "advisory" Q&A part toward a collaboration, which may look like more your peer-to-peer, unofficial RA. Active listening is already in your toolkit. Instead of trying to find out what the patron wants to read from what they are saying they want to read, you will focus on more subtle indicators throughout your dialog, such as the reader's reading experiences, current mood, and nonverbal cues. Your reward is more than just a collaborative effort to fulfill their need; these conversations might affect you too, or they might even trigger unexpected insights and revelations!

Keeping in mind the user first, book recommendations depend largely on the individual and their specific concerns and circumstances. The potential of turning an everyday situation into RA with bibliotherapeutic benefits might sound daunting at first. Over time, though, you can build your own skills for understanding your users' needs, such as reading nonverbal cues, asking follow-up questions to discern underlying personal concerns, picking up on and deftly handling reactions like embarrassment—in short, developing techniques to connect with the reader when they need it the most. You may want to keep a log of these experiences and the techniques you've developed, either shared with your staff or only for yourself. Writing down notes will help you process your experience and learn from it.

After many RA sessions and book recommendations, you may discover the benefits of the reciprocal nature of the process outside the RA dialog. It has quickly become second nature for many of us to read with an eye to a potential reader. Staff and librarians often recommend books to each other, but receiving reading suggestions from library users—why not? The reader with a special issue that has been bothering them might know a lot more about the related literature or any other material to distract, ponder, or find solutions. Take a look at some Goodreads threads for some inspiration.

It's okay to keep recommending the same book over and over again, if the situation warrants it. At the beginning of the pandemic, for example, one could see the same titles cropping up on multiple "corona reads" lists. However, approaching RA as a give-and-take between your recommendations and those of your users can expand your horizons for future interactions. If you haven't started yet, you can work on stepping out of your comfort zone when it comes to genres, authors, and formats—for example, try graphic novels or audiobooks.

An RA session inspired by bibliotherapy might just serve as the entry point for that user to discover and reflect on a whole new world. Why shouldn't you and your library benefit too? At a time when many library services are being asked to demonstrate their value or wind up on the chopping block, taking RA to the next level can provide evidence of your library's vital role in effective community outreach.

TABLE 4.1

Comparison Chart: Traditional Readers' Advisory (RA) and Bibliotherapy (BT)-Centered Readers' Advisory

	TRADITIONAL RA	BT-CENTERED RA
Definition	Suggesting books for recreational reading, fun, or self-education	Suggesting books to provide insight and motivation to read further and identify readers' own needs
Key features	Advisory Book oriented Attention to detail	Collaborative Reader oriented Holistic
Matching based on	How text appeals to reader	How text resonates with reader
Active format	One-on-one interview, building on the reader's previous reading experiences, likes, and dislikes	One-on-one reading experience conversation, building on the reader's mood and needs, perceived or real
Passive format	Reading lists, guides, websites, displays, browsable sources	Same as traditional RA, plus peer-to-peer book suggestion exchange, tagged online sources
Key interaction	The librarian and the reader during their interaction	The text and the reader after the librarian's guidance
Appeal factors	Book related—e.g., plot, storyline, narrative, character building, pacing, language, style, information need, reading level and experience	Reader driven—e.g., potential responses, emotions evoked, positive effects, resonance, level of need for support, self-perception, empathy, alternative perspectives, the reader's attitude to the text and to their own issues
Main emphasis	Books from the collection	Dialog between the librarian and the reader
Selection based on	What the reader says they want, based on their own words plus librarian judgment	What the reader may grow from, based on their own words plus librarian judgment

	TRADITIONAL RA	BT-CENTERED RA
Ultimate goal	Connecting a reader with a text to fulfill interest in established or new areas	Engaging the reader in a text, with a focus on mental and emotional involvement
Benefits for the reader	Pleasure reading; escapism, distraction, education; happy library user, personal growth	Discovery and transformation: the journey is more important than the destination
Benefits for the librarian	Serving the community, promoting the collection, connecting books and readers	All the traditional RA benefits, plus BT works both ways: "give and take" Personal growth

Group Discussions

Group discussions, whether synchronous (in person or online) or asynchronous (online only), are the most frequently used method of formal bibliotherapy led by a trained therapist. This is where your program will get interesting. There is no single way to run a group discussion. Trained bibliotherapists, psychologists, and counselors spend countless hours honing their skills, after hundreds of hours of supervised experience on how to run a session. To run a literary seminar in college, the instructor needs an advanced degree, usually either a PhD or progress toward one. A great author-talk moderator walks into the interview room with thousands of hours spent reading in general, and hundreds more reading that author's works and reflecting on them. We are not advising you to compete with any of these people, so don't feel intimidated!

In the group discussion, the "accidental bibliotherapist" librarian acts as a facilitator who connects the text with the reader. In this sense, an active bibliotherapy-inspired program can be placed somewhere between the reader-centered library and information science approach and the patient-centered psychology approach introduced in chapter 1—using literary texts rather than following a therapy manual, workbook, or self-help books. It's important to emphasize that librarians are not therapists. These group discussions are meant to complement traditional forms of therapeutic support, not to substitute for them. Moreover, if the opportunity presents itself, librarians in a discussion group might encourage the reader (discreetly, of course) to reach out to a licensed therapist. Chapter 7 will detail bibliotherapy-centered discussions.

Public Events

Large events, whether in the library or online, might seem intimidating, especially when dealing with sensitive subjects. We must admit that it took us a while to venture in this direction. The main reason to try is the extraordinary benefits these events provide: increased visibility for the library in the community with instant marketing opportunities and potential synergies.

Kicking off and wrapping up a program with scheduled events provides a framework for the program itself. Scoring a big name as a guest author does wonders for marketing, enhancing all your promotional efforts and granting more credibility to your program almost instantly.

If you have already hosted author talks or organized big events, you will know that the first large event can be tough, whether onsite or online. With thorough preparation, however, it will provide valuable experience that gives you both confidence in your abilities and trust in your partners in difficult situations, making the next event that much easier. Chapter 8 will present sample marketing and event schedules to customize to your program.

In a Nutshell

If you have any doubts about your competency to start a bibliotherapy-centered program in your library, this chapter functions both as inspiration to get started and as an inventory of your hidden skills that are translatable into active and passive modalities for bibliotherapy. The best part of bibliotherapy is its inherent diversity and versatility—from the book displays to the readers' advisory to the guest author readings that you have already been doing. Bibliotherapy can be an opportunity to design new programs or to retool existing ones like readers' advisory in order to better serve the needs of your community and forge new partnerships.

05 | Know Thy Audience

This chapter focuses on the part of bibliotherapy-inspired pro-grams that defines them the most: the participant. The success of your program depends on the target audience as much as on the book selection—perhaps even more so, as selecting titles that reach the reader would be impossible without getting to know them. Bibliotherapy-inspired programs have broad appeal—if you can adequately define your audience within your community. You will find ideas in this chapter on how to best match a book with its readers without any presupposition or predisposition.

We also advocate that the content and the structure of a bibliotherapy-inspired program work together, tailored to the needs and expectations of your potential audiences. This chapter presents examples and scenarios that allow you to set up a reading group of current patrons based on their background, their particular interests, or the phase of life they are in at the moment.

Matchmaking: The Right Book at the Right Time with the Right Framing

At its core, bibliotherapy is a way of thinking about the relationship between books and their readers. It's a practice founded on the recognition that books can "speak to" readers—that under the right circumstances, readers can find in books a new and helpful perspective on their own lives and concerns. As a result, bibliotherapy is the practice of bringing about those "right circumstances" by matching an appropriate book to its reader at a time when it can be of value.

The essential idea here is that there's no single, one-size-fits-all "right book" for everyone. It's more like matchmaking. Different books will work for different readers; one reader's trash is another's treasure. Just like a matchmaker, the bibliotherapist (professional or accidental) makes an educated guess based on their knowledge of both book and reader and sees if the sparks fly. For any given reader, there's probably at least a handful of books that might speak to them—but, like falling in love, when a great match comes along, it seems like destiny in hindsight, as though book and reader were made to meet each other at this moment.

If the goal of bibliotherapy is to facilitate such life-altering (or at least life-improving) matches between books and readers, then a bibliotherapy-informed approach to librarianship would start with understanding your patrons, community members, or target audience for possible programs. Subsequent chapters will discuss the selection of reading material and program design, but those are both contingent on the readers you're trying to reach. Remember, there is no one-size-fits-all "right book" for everyone—only good fits for particular people at particular moments. This chapter discusses some aspects you might consider when designing programs and selecting readings in order to have a solid shot at success.

Thinking Creatively: Opting for Greater Variety of Perspectives

Designing a program for a group will always be different from tailoring a reading recommendation to a specific individual, and it's important not to overemphasize demographics as a stand-in for the inner lives of participants. Shared characteristics—especially shared therapeutic needs, like a group for people with addictions—can help you choose readings and program structures that stand a good chance of working for their target audience.

It's important to choose books with characters, situations, and concerns that your participants can relate to and that may mirror characteristics like race, gender, cultural background, socioeconomic class, age, immigration status, or sexual orientation. Just seeing something of yourself reflected back in a book can be a powerful experience, especially for those of us from historically underrepresented groups. Plus, the concerns that books help readers reflect on are often intimately tied up with identity—protecting one's self-worth from racism, coming out as gay or trans, growing up between cultures, and so on. But the relationship between book and reader is much richer and stranger than an outward resemblance to the protagonist. Sometimes we read books to explore lives that are different from our own, and a connection can be all the more powerful when it comes from an unlikely place. It's best to think creatively, rather that deterministically, about what might speak to your audience. When in doubt, opt for a greater variety of perspectives.

To return to the matchmaking analogy, similar backgrounds can help facilitate a good match, but if someone dates only people exactly like themselves, they might miss out on a beautiful and life-changing relationship.

Defining Your Audience, Current and Potential

First, where will you find your audience for bibliotherapy-informed reading programs? The answer might seem obvious—among your library users, of course!—but it still bears some consideration. There are trade-offs involved in choosing your target audience, and your choice will also determine how you structure your program. Those trade-offs aren't always so obvious. A broadly targeted or generic program, open to all comers, will have the largest universe of possible participants, but no natural constituency; potential users will not necessarily feel that this program is meant for them and may be apprehensive about opening up to a group of strangers about whom they know nothing. In a K–12 school or university library where users already have something in common (i.e., being students at the same school), this is a little less of a concern; but no matter the community in question, program designers should keep in mind that the relationship between the specificity of the target audience and the likelihood of having enough participants may not be exactly linear.

It's important to consider not only current users as a possible audience, but potential users as well. A bibliotherapy-informed reading program can be a great opportunity for outreach—a chance to bring community members and groups into library programs for the first time, and perhaps create more regular users in the process. Are there groups in the community you serve who are not yet regular library users but might be drawn in by such a program? If so, how can you structure the program to attract them, and how will you make sure they know about it? Program designers might want to think here about groups that are already "library adjacent": those who may not be regular program participants but are familiar with the library, perhaps even using its physical space or other services. For a school library, these might be students who study or meet in the library on their own or use its online services; for a public library, these might be groups that use the library as a formal or informal meeting space. These groups will be easier to reach and more likely to participate. If catering to existing "usual suspects" for library programs is the safe option and attempting to bring in a completely different constituency offers a high reward with a higher risk of failure, using bibliotherapy-inspired programs to bring "library-adjacent" or occasional library users more fully and actively into the library community is a solid middle ground. (In any case, you can't assume that "if you build it, they will come"; we'll discuss how to market a program to potential audiences in further detail in chapters 9 and 10.)

It helps to think here about groups that already have some existing social structure or potential for word-of-mouth advertising. A reading group is a social group, and people will be more likely to join if they can sign up with a friend or at least know some fellow participants (in addition to meeting new people). A bibliotherapy-informed program will also require at least some trust among the participants themselves, which comes more naturally in groups that are tailored to those who share some background or life experience. The authors, for instance, have run or participated in bibliotherapy or bibliotherapy-informed groups for people in recovery, college students, and expats from a particular country. Even if participants in groups like these don't know each other coming in, they may be willing to be more vulnerable in these spaces because other participants will be more likely to relate.

It also helps when participants feel connected to, or feel they can trust, the facilitator. This is yet another reason it's good to have a diverse team that reflects the community you serve. However, this connection or trust doesn't have to come from a shared demographic or background—it's important not to limit your sights to participants who resemble you or your colleagues, particularly when the library's mission is to serve a diverse community! Think about how you and your team can leverage your existing ties to the community to get participants to take that initial leap of faith involved in signing up. After that, you can focus on continuing to earn their trust as a facilitator as the program goes on.

Serving Your Audience with Structure and Content

The better you know your audience, the better you will meet their needs, real or perceived, pressing or evolving alike. Nevertheless, your first few sessions might feel hit-and-miss, until you get to know who the people in the group are. A few pointers to consider before designing your program go a long way. You want to set it up not only to attract readers for a one-shot discussion (although a demo meeting has its own merits), but also to create a warm, welcoming, and safe environment that will remain sustainable throughout the program. The content you will use is defined by the format and structure of the group discussion, and these are based on the target audience.

Structuring Your Program

Once you've decided on your target audience, it's time to think about how to structure the program to best fit their needs. Will enough of them be willing and able to make regular meetings (either in person or online), or would they prefer the flexibility of an asynchronous format? For example, generally speaking, students at a residential college or retired seniors might be more likely to prefer regular meetings, while people who work multiple jobs or parents with young children (unless childcare is available) may find it hard to find consistent meeting times that work for enough group members to be worthwhile. If the group meets synchronously, the time of day matters as well. Evening hours are the only option for those working a traditional 9-to-5, for instance, and may be better for students as well so as not to conflict with classes, while stay-at-home parents with school-age children are more likely to be free during the day. Familiarity with or preexisting connections to the target audience can be helpful; if you don't know what members of your target audience would prefer, it's much easier if you can just ask them!

The other basic program decision is to choose between virtual and in-person modalities. Both present problems of access as well as preference. To state the obvious, a virtual discussion requires reliable internet access, which is increasingly common but still not universal. A virtual discussion is also accessible only to those with enough tech savvy to use a discussion board or virtual meeting platform—tools that are increasingly common in the post-pandemic world, especially among students and younger people, but still not familiar to everyone. Even those who can use these tools when necessary may not feel comfortable with them, and it's important that participants feel at ease rather than flustered or turned off by the technology. Many will simply prefer in-person conversation, especially after "Zoom fatigue" from the online-only pandemic environment.

PLATFORM PIGGYBACKING

Planning to set up your program on a platform that members of your target audience use routinely is probably the easiest way to reach them. You'd have instant visibility, an obvious marketing channel, and more opportunities to reach out.

For our Summer Tales reading club, we chose Canvas, the online learning management system used by students registered for any of the classes during the summer sessions. We did calculate the risks: a summer reading program that looks like a class might feel like school and homework—one more thing to do in a semester condensed into four to six weeks—and the platform might put a damper on all our brilliant ideas of how to engage students.

It worked nonetheless. The benefits surely far outweighed the risks. The novelty didn't wear off; moreover, students appreciated the convenience of the easy access. Canvas served as the platform for two more summer reading programs after the first one, even though Zoom fatigue became more and more palpable over the three summers.

In-person meetings have their own trade-offs. As we write this, COVID is still circulating and still dangerous, particularly to those with compromised immune systems or preexisting risk factors; some participants may require or strongly prefer the safety of virtual events as long as that remains the case. The pandemic has also revealed that when given the choice, many people just prefer the convenience of meeting virtually to the logistical hassle of a commute. Virtual meetings can ease the difficulty of arranging childcare or a ride. Some people might even find it easier to open up over a computer rather than face to face, particularly if that means they can compose their thoughts in writing via live chat or discussion boards—these participants may be more forthcoming when they don't have to speak off the cuff, or don't have to "speak" at all to participate. There's no right answer between in-person and virtual programs, only the better answer for a majority of your participants.

Finally, if you've opted for an asynchronous program, administering it virtually may be your only option. Synchronous groups can easily be either online or offline, but it's hard to imagine an asynchronous, in-person group with meaningful opportunities for engagement. If your target audience can't meet at the same time and won't meet online, you'll likely have to forgo group discussion and stick with passive resources such as reading lists and questions to reflect (though if you can find a creative solution, more power to you—perhaps a physical "discussion board" where participants can write down their thoughts, like a hotel guestbook?).

Content Matters

The choice of audience will inform not only program structure and modality, but also reading selections. We'll talk more about how to choose readings in the following chapter, but for now there are some specific considerations that the choice of audience will affect.

First, a word on "reading level": the concept isn't actually that helpful outside of grade school, and program designers are better off thinking about the specific preferences and needs of the target audience than risking false assumptions or trying to fit their differences into a one-size-fits-all container. For example: non-native speakers (including an author of this book!) or people with less formal education can be both very proficient and prolific readers, who might be insulted to be underestimated—and if they do struggle, it's likely to be with different aspects of texts. So, instead of thinking in terms of "reading level," consider instead whether there are any accessibility and approachability concerns that are particular to your audience—and no matter what, make sure never to come across as condescending when addressing these concerns. In most cases, err on the side of works that are relatively simple to read and complex in the questions they provoke. (See also the guidelines in chapter 6.)

The length of the readings you select might vary a little more based on the target audience, though here, too, we offer a rule of thumb: shorter is often better! Some participants, like those who work full-time and/or take care of children, may have very little time for pleasure reading and thus particularly prefer short selections, like a (very) short story or a poem. But no matter the audience, keeping the selections short will lower the barrier to entry to the group by reducing the time commitment. As a facilitator, you may be worried about not having enough to talk about, but the amount of discussion a text can yield doesn't have a direct relationship to its length any more than to the difficulty of its language. There are groups that enjoy reading longer texts, but unless you know yours is one of them—a preexisting book club, for instance—shorter texts tend to yield a better participation rate for any target audience.

If the difficulty and the length of the readings are actually less dependent on the target audience than you might expect, the subject matter will vary quite a bit more. Program designers will want to tailor readings to the audience, picking things they might enjoy and relate to. If your group is organized around a specific therapeutic concern, you could begin by collecting texts that address that concern head-on. When the authors put together a database of bibliotherapy texts for people with addictions, for instance, we began with memoirs and fictional depictions of addiction. If your bibliotherapy-informed program caters to a particular background or life experience—students, for instance, or new parents—you might begin by collecting literary texts that are about, or are written by, people of that group.

However, reading is all about making unanticipated connections! Readers often enjoy and find meaning in texts that don't depict people exactly like them or situations exactly like their own. In fact, as we'll discuss in the following chapter, one of the key insights of bibliotherapy is the value of indirection: the safety and potential for insight that comes from talking about someone else's story (real or fictional) rather than exclusively and directly about your own. Look for readings that provide fruitful areas of connection for your target audience, even if they don't seem similar on the surface, and trust your participants to get what they need from them—even if it's simply an opportunity to get out of their own heads and into someone else's for a time.

HOW PROUST CAN CHANGE YOUR LIFE

A title such as *In Search of Lost Time* (in seven volumes) by Marcel Proust is definitely not a lightweight weekend read. Nevertheless, in his book *How Proust Can Change Your Life: Not a Novel*, Alain de Botton managed to transform even Proust's writing into a self-help book. Our favorite quote:

> "We should read other people's books in order to learn what we feel; it's our own thoughts we should be developing, even if it's another writer's thoughts that help us do so."

Source: Alain de Botton, *How Proust Can Change Your Life: Not a Novel*, 1st ed. (New York: Pantheon, 1997), 178.

That principle of strategic indirection cuts both ways: not only is there value in choosing readings that offer unanticipated connections, but it can also actually be best to choose readings that aren't too close for comfort, particularly when dealing with painful or traumatic experiences. One of the advantages of bibliotherapy is that it allows participants to process part of the therapeutic experience privately, while reading, before bringing it up with others; it's especially important in a group setting to allow participants the option to maintain some distance from overwhelming feelings or reliving trauma. Choosing readings that are close enough for connection without being too close for comfort is part of allowing your participants to manage that distance for themselves, which is both a key advantage of a bibliotherapy-informed approach and a key distinction from a clinical group therapy setting—a distinction that an "accidental bibliotherapist," as an information services professional rather than a mental health professional, must always be careful to maintain.

Rounding Up Potential Audiences

Each library has its own audience, whether primary or secondary. Here follow a few examples of library patrons who can easily form a reading group based on their background, interest, or current phase of life. Subgroups within these populations can also be mixed and matched, such as young adults who are also non-native speakers of English or senior citizens living alone.

Senior Citizens

Seniors can be a great audience for reading programs. Because they are more likely to be retired and lack childcare responsibilities, they may have more flexible schedules than other groups, including free time during the day. They are also likely to be a preassembled audience, so to speak: many communities already have programs targeted at seniors, perhaps even a senior center, or even just public spaces where they informally congregate (including the library). The combination of being more likely to have free time during the day and comfortable with in-person sessions seems like a natural fit, though as always be wary of assumptions: some seniors may be very comfortable with computers, much more so than the elders of past decades, and some may prefer remote sessions (especially those who have mobility issues and/or lack reliable transportation). Content for this group can vary widely; aging is a natural concern that bibliotherapy can address, but with a wide range of life experiences to draw on, seniors may be interested in and able to relate to any number of topics. With this group in particular, it may be helpful to choose texts that are available in multiple formats so that those with vision impairments can participate with large-print or audiobook options.

RECOMMENDED READ FOR SENIORS

"Diem Perdidi"

For a story about aging, we recommend Julie Otsuka's "Diem Perdidi," a compelling, heart-wrenching portrait of an elderly woman's character and life story as she begins to lose her memory. The story invites us to reflect on what makes up individual identity—our experiences, our habits, our relationships—and what happens to them when they slip out of our grasp. Be advised that for participants affected by their own or a loved one's memory loss, it may hit close to home. (See appendix B for a sample discussion guide.)

College Students

For a college or university library, students are a perfect prebuilt audience: a large local group with shared characteristics, relatively strong internal ties (from classes and other activities together), and even a comprehensive email list! Reading groups can be a great way to get students who already use library facilities to start participating in library programs as well, and even nudge those who have previously used only the physical space and public computing to start exploring the collections. Coming-of-age stories work particularly well for this group. Don't be afraid to mix up selections, though; the university setting is all about broadening students' horizons, and many will be eager to read about something new and unfamiliar. In-person sessions are relatively easy to put together during the school year, especially on primarily residential campuses, whereas online sessions are a natural choice during the summer, when students (and librarians) are less likely to be taking in-person classes. Keep selections short, especially for programs during the semester—students are likely to have plenty of reading to do already!

RECOMMENDED READ FOR COLLEGE STUDENTS

"How to Talk to Girls at Parties"

For a coming-of-age story by an author many students will already know, try Neil Gaiman's "How to Talk to Girls at Parties," which the authors have had success with. Gaiman uses hints of supernatural forces at work to capture the anxiety and confusion of being a teenager, trying to play it cool when you're only dimly aware of what's really going on. (See appendix B for a sample discussion guide.)

People in Recovery

Among groups organized around specific therapeutic concerns, people in recovery from addictions stand out as already having a peer-support infrastructure and (particularly in twelve-step programs) an emphasis on sharing and relating to stories. There are plenty of fictional and nonfictional accounts of addiction out there, though, as with any traumatic experience, care should be taken to avoid overwhelming participants—the goal is a safe and controlled exploration, not a sudden plunge back to one's lowest points. A bibliotherapy-informed reading program is a complement to, rather than a substitute for, the potentially intense clinical setting of individual or group therapy. Works that deal with addiction obliquely, either as one part of a story among others or as a possible allegory, can fill an important role here, allowing participants to choose their preferred level of vulnerability.

RECOMMENDED READ FOR PEOPLE IN RECOVERY

"Sleeping and Waking"

F. Scott Fitzgerald's "Sleeping and Waking" is a short story about insomnia that both hints at and potentially allegorizes alcohol addiction. Anyone who has dealt with thoughts and anxieties they can't quite keep out of mind—especially during those late hours when there's nothing else to block them out—will feel like it's their experience too. (See appendix B for a sample discussion guide.)

Immigrants (and/or English Language Learners)

Immigrants and/or English language learners may be particularly interested in joining a program that offers both a social support group of similar individuals and a chance to explore questions of language and culture—something literature is especially well suited for. With these groups, it's especially helpful to think about the characteristics of the community and how specifically targeted the program should be. In addition to the important distinction between immigrants and English language learners (groups with significant overlap that are nonetheless not identical), immigrants might also have different experiences based on their age at immigration, their country or region of origin, and so on. Participants may feel most at home when they have some characteristics in common, but it can also be rewarding for them to discover unexpected cross-cultural or cross-generational connections. For this reason, it may work best to target the group broadly at first and then tailor the experience based on who signs up.

RECOMMENDED READ FOR IMMIGRANTS

"Persimmons"

Li-Young Lee's poem "Persimmons" is a wonderful choice for exploring themes of growing up between languages and cultures. The poem tracks a coming-of-age tale through an associative logic, bringing together the feeling of foreignness in an elementary school classroom, connecting with a first love, and caring for an aging parent through the motif of the persimmon. (See appendix B for a sample discussion guide.)

In a Nutshell

One of the benefits of any directed reading program is that it can be designed with the library's community in mind. You can thus help participants see themselves reflected in the chosen text or expose them to new perspectives. There are many ways to get to know your community even when you are one of them. This chapter encourages you to know the target audience to best tailor your program's structure and reading selections. As you learn more and more about both your books and your users—while narrowing your audience down to a manageable group—you'll experience how your choices inform and define the structure and preferred modalities of your program along with the reading selections.

PART III

Getting to Work

06 | Selecting Reading Material

Selecting reading material can be the most time-intensive part of creating your program. There's so much out there that even once you limit your selection to a targeted search, or to only those materials held in your library, you can spend whole days reading and hardly make a dent in the pile. If that sounds like heaven to you (as it does to us), don't let us stop you! Your search for readings can be as short or as long, within reason, as you want it to be. This chapter will equip you to make that search more productive by offering some general principles on the kinds of readings you'll want to look for, where to look, how to apply your criteria, and how to present your reading list for participants.

How to Select Reading Material

The classic board game Othello was marketed under the slogan "A minute to learn, a lifetime to master." That about sums up the most important quality of a good reading selection: it should be approachable for everyone in the group to read and inexhaustible to discuss. All participants should be able to "get something out of" the selection, without running out of things to talk about. If the reading seems to point toward a single idea (like a specific "lesson" or "moral"), losing your interest once that has been grasped, it's probably not an ideal choice for a discussion.

A good discussion takes the unresolved questions and observations that participants can't quite figure out what to do with and builds them into new insights; if everything in the text seems self-explanatory and tidily wrapped up, it may not offer enough material to work with. You cannot

AT A GLANCE

■ How to Select Reading Material
■ Thoughts on Sensitivity

know for certain how your participants will respond to a text. It's always possible—even likely—that they'll come up with interesting questions and observations that didn't occur to you. What you're looking for, though, is what's sometimes called a "rich" text, one that offers a lot of potential entry points for interpretation and discussion. If you can see how the discussion might begin but not where it will end up, that's a sign that you've made a good choice!

On the other hand, if you have no idea where to begin with a text, chances are your participants won't either. This can be for any reason: because the vocabulary or syntax is too difficult, because the reader can't tell what's going on, because it seems to require background knowledge that participants might not have, or simply because you as the facilitator simply don't have anything to say about it. If you don't know what to do with it, chances are your participants won't either—especially since part of your role will be modeling engagement with the text. Above all, throughout the screening process, try not to beat yourself up over "not understanding" potential selections. Instead, think about whether this is a fruitful kind of non-understanding, where you would have things to talk about, or a dead-end kind where you wouldn't. If it's the latter case, it's not because there's anything wrong with you, or necessarily wrong with the text; it just doesn't speak to you. It's important to pick texts that speak to you, especially if you'll be actively facilitating the group. So when you come across one that doesn't, let it go and move on to the next.

Building on the "A minute to learn, a lifetime to master" theme, we particularly recommend using short stories or poems for bibliotherapy-focused discussion groups. The first and most obvious reason is that the shorter a text, the more likely participants will have enough time to read it thoroughly. Even in a college course, students might have a hard time reading a long novel. This is all the more true for a purely optional reading program, where participants may have full-time jobs or family duties (and where you can't assign quizzes or papers!). Participants may join in part because they find it hard to fit reading into their daily schedules and are looking for a structure to help them do so; keeping the reading load manageable is part of meeting them halfway. If you do assign a longer text, try to split it into smaller chunks for each session. In addition, if the story or poem is especially short, even students who haven't managed to do the reading before the group meets can read it over during the session. You can even opt for "self-contained" sessions with no preparation required, where the first five or ten minutes are allotted for participants to read or reread the text before beginning to discuss it. This can make the program more appealing for participants by not giving them "homework" to keep track of and can make discussions more productive as well because the text will be fresh in everyone's minds.

That brings us to the second reason to opt for shorter texts: they can sometimes lead to better discussions because they're small enough to hold in mind all at once and it's easier to refer back to specific moments in the text. At risk of being too literal, it's easier for everyone to be on the same page in discussion when there are fewer pages to begin with. Look for short poems and "flash fiction," a term sometimes used for especially short short stories.

Browsing the stacks is always a fun way to spend time, but there are other ways of finding potential readings.

DIVERSITY, EQUITY, AND INCLUSION IN TEXT SELECTION

Bearing in mind that libraries have long served as a place to practice freedom to read and speak, selection criteria for a bibliotherapy program should consider a diversity of authors and perspectives. This includes highlighting authors of underrepresented backgrounds; patrons from a similar background may be glad to see themselves represented in library programs, and others will benefit from encountering a new perspective. Diversity isn't just limited to broad demographics, however. It's impossible to represent every possible background, and moreover, diversity, equity, and inclusion have to do with the content as well as who is speaking.

It can help to consider your selections as a group and how they come together. Is there a clearly missing perspective here—an LGBTQIA+ perspective in a collection on relationships, for instance? Do selections from underrepresented groups seem siloed from the main list or like part of a shared conversation? For instance, while addressing racism is important, you don't want that to seem like the only and exclusive task of authors of color on your list. Ideally, your selections will be framed so that they "speak to" each other rather than being restricted to only "speaking for" a specific identity group.

Crowdsource

Readers are typically more than happy to share their recommendations! Friends, family, fellow librarians, social media contacts—anyone who reads— are likely to have something for you. Or why not ask your prospective participants directly? Having a favorite work on the agenda can be a great way to increase buy-in. You can certainly just ask people if they have anything to recommend, but to jog their memories you might want to consider more specific questions: What's the last work that changed your perspective in a meaningful way? What's a work you think everyone should read? What's the most interesting/helpful thing you've read on [topic X]?

Book Reviews

Published book reviews can be a great way to get ideas for potential readings. They are indispensable for staying up on recently published works and offer a layer of vetting (though no substitute for reading the work oneself before making a final selection). Keep an eye out in particular for "best of the year" lists in some of the below outlets or other special awards. Whether you browse the usual sources for potential library acquisitions, such as *Booklist, Kirkus Reviews, Library Journal, Publishers Weekly*, and *School Library Journal*, or read book reviews in *The New York Times*, with your new focus on bibliotherapy, it will be easy to keep an eye out for titles related to mental health and wellness topics relevant in your community.

Literary Magazines

Short stories and poems are often first published in magazines—a handful of general-interest magazines such as *Harper's* or *The New Yorker*, and a wide array of literary magazines such as *Granta* or *Ploughshares*. Browsing through the back issues of these magazines, in paper or online, can be a great way to find poems and short fiction. Note that these magazines will typically require a subscription in order to read.

The Poetry Foundation (www.poetryfoundation.org), which publishes *Poetry* magazine, deserves special mention here for its wide, well-curated, and free online repository of poems. The site has poems from every era of the distant past to the present day and offers collections on a particular topic that can be an excellent way to discover new poetry.

Select Databases

Many databases are usually subscription based. However, online booklists and recommendations can be helpful in finding the next potential biblio-therapy-related title for you and your readers since you are well versed in searching these databases. Databases can require a subscription, such as Bowker's Books in Print, EBSCO's NoveList, Gale Books and Authors, and Shelf Awareness, but many of them are available free of charge, such as Adult Reading Round Table, EarlyWord, RA for All, Whichbook, and, last but not least, a source called Biblio or Therapy? An Annotated Bibliography on Bibliotherapy for Librarians, which includes book recommendations.

SELECTING FOR GROUPS

"Adolescence-II"

For a group of college students, we chose Rita Dove's "Adolescence-II," a poem about the disorienting and bewildering experience of being a teenager. The speaker sits alone in the bathroom at night, where three supernatural visitors—"seal men"—appear and ask her, cryptically, if she can "feel it" yet. She doesn't know how to answer, and they laugh and disappear. The poem never says what "it" is, but the title suggests that "it" is something to do with the changes of adolescence or puberty. Here was some of the thought behind our selection:

Positives:

- It's a very short text, written in accessible language—students could easily fit it into their busy lives.
- Students would be more likely to respond to a work about an experience almost all of them had gone through recently.
- The poem's vivid imagery and air of mystery offered some easy jumping-off points for discussion: What do you think is happening here? What was an image that stood out to you, and why?

Potential negatives and our responses:

- The cryptic quality of the poem might turn off readers who want a more straightforward message. We decided that in a university environment, participants would be more likely to be comfortable with an open-ended, challenging selection.
- The poem alludes to sexuality, which might make some participants uncomfortable—the "it" that the speaker doesn't know whether she "feels yet" or not might be sexual arousal. We decided that while this interpretation is available, the poem doesn't insist on it, and so we could easily let the comfort level of our participants dictate the course of the discussion.

The selection turned out to be successful; participants seemed to relate to the feelings of unease that the poem depicted, without that awkwardness and unease coming out in the discussion! But your mileage may vary. As an English professor, one of the authors has taught this poem in four different college classrooms as well, sometimes to great success and sometimes to blank stares and awkward silences. Some students listed it as a favorite poem from the semester; others didn't care for it at all.

You can't be completely sure how a given selection will go over because that is ultimately up to your participants. All you can do is put yourself in the best position to succeed while also recognizing that not every text will strike a chord with every person. If you put thought and care into your selection, your participants will be more likely to show up and engage with the texts and more likely to recognize and appreciate your effort even if a given text doesn't quite work for them. To paraphrase the famous serenity prayer, try to control the things you can, let go of those you can't, and recognize where your control ends and the unpredictable, beautiful encounter between text and reader begins.

Thoughts on Sensitivity

The thought may have crossed your mind already: What about the possibility that a reading selection might hurt, offend, or upset a patron? The topics that are most important and salient in our lives, as well as in literature, also tend to be very personal and sensitive—issues of identity, of belonging, of injustice. These are both the things that matter most and the things that can be difficult, even painful, to talk or read about.

There are no perfect answers to these problems. A bibliotherapeutic approach, however, can at least offer some helpful ways to think about sensitivity in reading selection.

- *Recommendations are not endorsements, but they are a kind of care.* Librarians rightly say that having a book in their collection does not mean endorsing everything it says. Recommending a book to a person or a group does not mean a total endorsement either, but it does imply something more than merely having that book on your shelf. When you recommend something, you're saying, in effect, "I think this will be helpful for you in some way"—whether that's intellectual interest, emotional support, enjoyment, or another reason. Bibliotherapy focuses us on what people *do* with books and reminds us that making a recommendation is not only a judgment about how "good" a book is, but about how *useful* it might be for the person you're recommending it to. Think about your selections in this way: how might they be useful to your patron or patrons, and is there anything that's likely to get in the way of them being useful? A book can be good, even great, without being ideal for every reader and in every context.

- *The message isn't all that matters.* If a reader is a survivor of sexual violence, for instance, a book with graphic depictions of such abuse might be difficult for that person to read, even if the book condemns it. In addition to reliving their own experience, that survivor might also take issue with the way the book depicts sexual violence, even while agreeing with the overall message—perhaps the violence comes across as sensationalized, mined for cheap thrills or trite lessons. Different readers might have different reactions to whether a given piece of media is portraying traumatic material in a responsible way, see, for instance, the robust conversation over a TV show like *Game of Thrones*. This isn't a reason to avoid difficult topics altogether. But when assessing a possible reading selection, think beyond its stated message and instead about how people who have faced the issues described might read it. Would they be likely to find it sensitive and respectful, or exploitative?
- *Be aware of the three zones: comfort, risk, and danger.* Perhaps you've seen some version of this diagram before—if the "comfort zone," where we spend most of our lives, is dry land, and the "danger zone" is the sea, the "risk zone" (aka the "growth zone" or "stretch zone") is the shoreline in between (see figure 6.1). In the same way that we learn best in school when presented with material that's right at the edge of our comprehension, personal growth happens when we encounter ideas and situations that are challenging without being overwhelming. Therapy is all about helping people confront difficult issues—including traumatic experiences—in a way that feels safe and controlled. Guided reading can be similar, in its own way: a space in which difficult content can be made manageable because the reader has more control over the experience. Think about ways to foster that controlled engagement with difficult topics—rather than trying to avoid any such topics altogether on the one hand, or shock and overwhelm readers on the other.
- *You can't control everything.* Readers will make their own meaning from what they read and will do so in ways you can't anticipate. You cannot control the results of your selections—how readers will encounter the works you've chosen—but you can control the process. Think seriously about how readers of different backgrounds and life experiences might respond to your selections as you make them. If a reader takes issue

with one of your selections, try not to be defensive. Their comments could turn out to be the beginning of an interesting discussion—as long as they feel that their concerns are listened to and respected.

FIGURE 6.1
Comfort-growth-danger zones

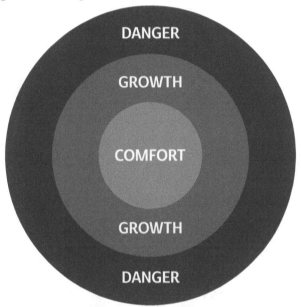

DANGER

GROWTH

COMFORT

GROWTH

DANGER

ASK THE EXPERT

MARIA ORTIZ-MYERS
Selecting for Parents of Gender-Diverse Children

Maria Ortiz-Myers is a PhD candidate in library and information science at the School of Communication and Information at Rutgers University–New Brunswick.

I focus on information practice in my doctoral research—in particular, personally meaningful information experiences. My dissertation explores how families of transgender youth pursue and assess information. This work has revealed some of the emotional salience of gender-related information, the information marginalization these families experience, and the identity-related information management parents and children perform.

People curious about this have asked me what parents read or what I recommend to anyone wanting to learn more about gender-diverse children. I have accumulated a few types of books, chiefly things that describe other research studies like mine.

For a précis of the early research into biogenetic aspects of sex and gender expression, I recommend *How Sex Changed: A History of Transsexuality in the United States* by Joanne Meyerowitz, *Gender: A Genealogy of an Idea* by Jennifer Germon, and Susan Stryker's classic *Transgender History: The Roots of Today's Revolution* (there is now a second edition). *Histories of the Transgender Child* by Jules Gill-Peterson is another fascinating account of chiefly early twentieth-century research in the US. I found it a challenging read because I have little background in the kind of work that Gill-Peterson does, but it is full of accounts taken from the Johns Hopkins University medical archives.

The stories that children, young people, and their parents tell about navigating their understanding of gender are essential and very moving. One of my favorite books in this vein is Ann Travers's *The Trans Generation: How Trans Kids (and Their Parents) Are Creating a Gender Revolution*. Travers writes about the families she met doing research, but the book is an affecting narrative and doesn't read as typical academic tome. Another great book—again, telling stories from dissertation research—is Tey Meadow's *Trans Kids: Being Gendered in the Twenty-First Century*. Meadow's language is a bit more academic, but this book is well worth the effort.

For families and parents interested in the emotional journey and the acceptance process, there is a choice to make. I tend to recommend some of the guides for counseling professionals. A few great ones are *Families in Transition: Parenting Gender Diverse Children, Adolescents, and Young Adults*, edited by Arlene I. Lev and Andrew R. Gottlieb, *The Transgender Child: A Handbook for Families and Professionals* by Stephanie Brill and Rachel Pepper, and either *Gender Born, Gender Made: Raising Healthy Gender-Nonconforming Children* or *The Gender Creative Child: Pathways for Nurturing and Supporting Children Who Live Outside Gender Boxes*, both by Diane Ehrensaft. My shelf doesn't have many memoirs, except for *Becoming Nicole* by Amy Ellis Nutt. I could discuss many more titles, but these are the ones I return to most often.

I have an "up next" side of my shelf that I want to mention. I have started but not finished *The Bold World* by Jodie Patterson. I like it a lot, and it is the only account written about a Black family by a Black woman. Gill-Peterson points out in their book that trans research is astonishingly concentrated on middle-class white families, while Black trans folks suffer more violence than others. I also looking forward to reading *Growing Up Queer: Kids and the Remaking of LGBTQ Identity* by Mary Robertson and *Beyond Trans: Does Gender Matter?* by Heath Fogg Davis.

In a Nutshell

Selecting material is probably one of the most enjoyable parts of the job as a librarian, whether for your collection or a program. If you are one of those susceptible to going down rabbit holes about a topic, author, and genre, welcome to the club! You can rely on your intellectual curiosity, plus your intimate knowledge of your collection and your library users in addition to the guidelines discussed in this chapter. Just find that "ideal" book—the one close to your vision that fits well with your audience—and start experimenting. Remember, it's not only about the text. The participants will bring just as much to the conversation as the author, if not more.

07 | Setting Up Bibliotherapy- Infused Programs

If you have experience hosting book clubs in the library or on your own, you have a pretty good idea of what you are getting into; if not, there's no time like the present to start! This chapter prepares librarians for running group discussions and events—including stressing the importance of preparation itself. A bibliotherapy perspective provides a new wrinkle on the classic model, adding a little difficulty to the preparation but a lot of reward to the result. Here we detail pre-event, behind-the-scenes activities, such as how to create a background guide, which contains more information about the topic or text and is primarily for your own use, and a discussion guide, which is more for public consumption and includes some of the same background information along with the discussion questions. We also present best practices for moderating a conversation, ensuring confidentiality, and establishing ground rules.

Running a Group Discussion

As anyone who has taught will know, fostering a conversation that feels free flowing and spontaneous actually requires a lot of preparatory work behind the scenes.

In a 1956 lecture at Oxford, W. H. Auden claimed that his approach as a literary critic starts with two basic lines of inquiry. The first is about style: How does this "verbal contraption" work? How does it say what it says, how does it interact with its reader? The second is about the textual

AT A GLANCE

- Running a Group Discussion
- Background Guides
- Background Research: Principles and Best Practices
- Discussion Guides
- Discussion Principles
- Guiding Participants to a Great Discussion
- Troubleshooting: Avoiding and Reacting to Participant Distress or Conflict

world and its characters: What sort of a person "inhabits" this work? What does he or she aspire toward, fear, conceal?[1]

Each of these angles is meant to elicit not definitive answers, but observations that can lead to connections. A text is above all a constructed world, as seen from a certain point of view, and getting really acclimated to another world takes time and attention. A discussion starts with noticing: "I found it hard to be sure why X acts this way." "This story jumps around in time a lot." "Y seems like a really important moment here." Each of these is an implicit opportunity for further questioning: How does the text do this, or why? In fact, articulating a question can be just as valuable to a discussion as providing an answer.

You probably have some experience in leading discussions, whether in the library or the classroom. Table 7.1 summarizes a few elements that bibliotherapy-centered programs may add to a traditional discussion.

TABLE 7.1

Discussions in Traditional and Bibliotherapy-Centered Programs

	TRADITIONAL	BT-CENTERED
Goal	Discuss a book, story, or text for pleasure during the session	Reflect on texts for individual therapeutic benefits after session
Background research	Some needed	Extensive research strongly recommended
Synopsis/ teaser	Storyline summarized; can be from the publisher	Your own, to frame discussion
Questions to use	Can be from the publisher, mixed with your own	Always your own questions, with talking points tailored to the group
Discussion process	Talk about the "what"—plot, events, characters	Talk about the "how" experience, especially "how the reader sees it"
Takeaway for participants	About the world; could include new knowledge, new interests	About themselves; potential insights rather than "lessons" or "messages"

Background Guides

The main resource for a bibliotherapy-centered program is the collection of data that a librarian can pull together from available sources that we call a "background guide," full of information about the topic, author, text, and more that might be relevant to the target audience. Background guides—working as both a direct reference tool and an inspiration to find out more about the text and the author—are incredibly useful for your participants, and for you too.

You may wonder how a bibliotherapy-centered guide would be different from a traditional one. Perhaps the most obvious difference is the focus on the therapeutic issue or issues under consideration. Psychological, medical, sociological, and other specialized texts from the healing arts or social sciences might be included to flesh out the portrait of a specific condition or concern. A short story about Alzheimer's, for example, like Alice Munro's "The Bear Came Over the Mountain" or Julie Otsuka's "Diem Perdidi," could be usefully contextualized with some approachable medical literature about memory loss and some social science articles on how it affects sufferers and their loved ones.

Remember, however, not to overmedicalize in your background guide: not all therapeutic concerns can (or should) fit into a diagnosis. And even for those that can, part of the point of bibliotherapy is to explore the dimensions of experience that don't fit neatly into an intake form or a DSM questionnaire! The *therapy* in *bibliotherapy*, particularly in its developmental form, is less narrowly focused on treating a specific ailment than on processing the full range of human experience, good, bad, and in between. The isolation associated with the immigrant experience, for instance, is a rich therapeutic topic that doesn't fit into a diagnostic box, nor should it—being an immigrant is not a "condition" to be "treated" but an aspect of one's identity and a way of being in the world.

Even when there is a medical tie-in to a reading, sometimes overemphasizing the medical aspect in a background guide can lead to an unsatisfying game of pin-the-diagnosis-on-the-character or, much worse, replicate stigma by reducing an identity to an illness. If the reading is about a transgender or nonbinary person, for example, the background guide should be careful not to exclusively focus on gender dysphoria: even if the resources are compassionate and sympathetic, such a framework harkens back to the not-distant-enough days when nonmajority sexualities and gender identities were considered mental illnesses rather than normal varieties of the human experience. The best way is to cultivate a number of approaches in your background resources, to avoid polemical frameworks, and to err on the side of normalizing therapeutic concerns and fleshing out what they are like to experience.

If the reading in question touches on sensitive topics that might hit close to home for some readers, it's a good idea to include a brief note. We would advise against thinking of this like a parental advisory sticker or an allergen notice (or letting it resemble one in style). These notes shouldn't be a scarlet letter, marking out these texts as "difficult" or "controversial"; the very fact that a topic can be sensitive or personal makes it that much more important to talk about, and often means that talking about it openly and compassionately can have therapeutic value. Think of these notes as a kind of preparation, a heads-up so that readers don't feel blindsided. Some may opt out of such topics, while others will be eager for the opportunity to discuss them. Either way, a note will rarely go amiss. Don't worry about spoilers—avoiding unpleasant surprises is much more important than cultivating suspense!

SAMPLE BACKGROUND GUIDE

"Eight Bites" by Carmen Maria Machado
Carmen Maria Machado spins a slightly surreal, quietly affecting tale of a woman's bariatric surgery, exploring the connections between food, family, femininity, and body image.

About the Story
In "Eight Bites," Carmen Maria Machado explores the mind of a woman who undergoes bariatric weight loss surgery. It's often said that food is family, and the relationship of Machado's narrator to food and her own body is refracted through her relationships with the women of her family: an iron-willed mother, gossipy sisters, and a concerned daughter. Weaving realistic storytelling with a surrealist twist, Machado explores the complicated feelings around

a simple clinical procedure: desire, shame, love, envy, and a sense of having "lost" something more than merely weight.

Note to Readers
This story deals with difficult topics, including body shame and fraught relationships to food and family. One of the advantages of a remote, asynchronous discussion is that participants who feel uncomfortable can step away without any kind of disruption, and we encourage you to take advantage of that if things start to hit too close to home.

About the Discussion
We ask you to be mindful during the discussion of how personal this topic can be. Consider how someone else might interpret a comment you're making before posting it; for instance, someone struggling with weight or body image might take your well-intentioned fitness tips as implying that they've never tried these things before, or that there's something inherently wrong with a body they've worked hard to accept. We also want to suggest caution about sharing painful personal memories and making these the focus of discussion. Keeping the focus on the story instead allows us to touch on these important topics while maintaining a little bit of distance from the raw nerves of our own personal histories. After all, that's part of what fiction is for.

About the Book
Her Body and Other Parties (Graywolf, 2017) is a short story collection by Carmen Maria Machado. It won the 2017 Shirley Jackson Award and was a finalist for the 2017 National Book Award for Fiction. The story "The Husband Stitch" was nominated for the 2014 Nebula Award for Best Novelette. (Source: Wikipedia.)

About the Author
Carmen Maria Machado (born 1986) is an American short story author, essayist, and critic frequently published in *Granta*, *Lightspeed Magazine*, *The New Yorker*, and other publications. She has been a finalist for the National Book Award and the Nebula Award for Best Novelette. Her stories have been reprinted in *Best Weird*

Fiction, Best American Science Fiction & Fantasy, Best Horror of the Year, The New Voices of Fantasy, and *Best Women's Erotica*. Her memoir *In the Dream House* was published in 2019. Machado lives in Philadelphia with her wife. (Source: Wikipedia.)

- Carmen Maria Machado's author page includes biography, writings, interviews, events, media, and more: https://carmenmariamachado.com/
- Carmen Maria Machado's homepage at the Department of English, University of Pennsylvania: https://www.english.upenn.edu/people/carmen-maria-machado

Background Research: Principles and Best Practices

Librarians are, among other things, experts in research. Putting together a background guide on a chosen text is a perfect opportunity to put those skills to use for your bibliotherapy-focused program too. Anything can serve as a background guide—from a rich but messy, in-house, staff-only resource, to a public-facing author guide such as a LibGuide. Here are some factors to consider adding to it, along with content and issues to address.

Sample Resources for Background Research

- "The Usual Suspects": Books, book reviews, biographies, scholarly publications, library catalog, author's homepage, WorldCat, LibGuides
- Related content: general internet search, author's fan page, publisher's page, vendor records, Goodreads, YouTube, social media resources

Ideas for Headlines to Post in Public-Facing Background Guides

- About: the story, poem, author, book, or topic to provide content details
- Resources from the library: reviews, scholarly articles, other titles by the same author, related reading to promote the library

- Quotes: inspirational, thoughtful, or representative quotes from the text discussed or other notable quotes by the author to set the tone
- Fun: videos, podcasts, and interviews with the author to add more value

Discussion Guides

One of the most useful tools we have developed are discussion guides: lists of questions that help guide the conversation in productive directions. The discussion guide may include some of the same material as the background guide, but it differs in at least two important ways: (1) philosophically, it is tailored toward the discussion session rather than the experience of reading on one's own; and (2) practically, this means that it will include suggested discussion questions.

Aside from being tailored toward the discussion, the discussion sheets are open ended: facilitators can use these lists of questions as a private "cheat sheet," circulate them ahead of time for participants to consider, or even circulate them in lieu of a live session as a suggested framework for participants to have their own discussions. Drawing upon your first few discussion guides, you may want to create a template. (See appendix B for an example.)

In our experience, four to six questions work well—enough that it's possible to shift gears if one avenue of discussion proves unproductive, but not so many as to take the weight off individual questions or to lead participants to move on too quickly. Below are the key elements to create a discussion guide, including, most important of all, tips on how to ask strong questions.

The Synopsis

Our discussion guides often begin with a short description of the text. This is meant to jog participants' memories, but it can also serve to subtly frame the discussion. Be careful to avoid definitive statements (e.g., "This story teaches us X" or "This character represents Y") that might shut down productive avenues of conversation.

The Author Bio

If you include this section, keep it short and largely focused on the work. A common way for discussions of literary texts to get bogged down is in speculating about the author's personal history and inner life—we simply can't know (or at least can't provide enough information in a short biographical sketch to guess). If, say, a difficult family relationship or a specific political climate is important background knowledge for your bibliotherapy-focused discussion, mention it here, but take care to keep the discussion questions focused on what we can know from the text itself.

Questions

A good first question will collect participants' first impressions of the text: What moments in particular struck them? Or: What kind of mood did the text convey? Make sure to keep this open ended, rather than asking participants to jump right away to what it all means.

- You might also begin by asking participants about what they found relatable in the text. Be careful, though, to keep the focus on the text itself, particularly early on in the discussion. Bibliotherapy allows participants to process their personal experiences, but through the *shared* and *safe medium* of the text. This is the important distinction between bibliotherapy discussion and traditional group therapy, which is a different matter and requires professional training most librarians don't have. Keep the main focus of the exercise on the text—*what* participants found relatable in the reading, rather than the similar experiences they may have had.
- In follow-up questions, think about specific moments in the text that you can focus attention on: interesting plot points, or even unconventional word choices. Quote specific language or refer to specific incidents in your question.
- At least a couple of questions should point to specific points in the text. These can be related to or build on each other, or not. You can also view these questions pointing to specific moments as striking a match, trying to spark a discussion—if one doesn't do the trick, or the discussion peters out, try another!

- The final question or questions should not ask participants to sum up the entire text or its "message." Instead, think of this as a kind of coda or outro to a piece of music, picking up on the themes of the discussion in a new light.

Discussion Principles

Facilitating a bibliotherapy-themed discussion requires quite a bit of flexibility because every discussion is different: participants will be interested in different things, the particular personalities involved will mesh in different ways, and so on. Even the same group can have a different dynamic from one meeting to another. A facilitator's job is to help keep the conversation moving in ways that participants find productive, which requires both a feel for the room and a sense of when and how to step in, nudging the conversation in productive directions without crowding out participation. These are difficult skills, but ones that improve with practice. Here are some general tips to keep in mind:

- Participants should not feel compelled to jump to the "point" or "lesson" of the text right away. Philosophically speaking, the text doesn't contain the "lesson"; if anything, the discussion does.
- In this setting, personal experience is part of how participants process the text, and the text is part of how participants process personal experience. If you feel that the conversation has stagnated or participants are talking past each other, it may be because the text as a shared ground has dropped out of the conversation. In this case, you might want to subtly redirect the conversation back to the text, perhaps by connecting someone's contribution to a specific moment in the reading.
- Often the most productive way to focus a discussion is to linger on a particularly complex, weighty passage. Ask: What does it mean? What sticks out to you here? What's the role of this passage in the work as a whole, and what does it connect to?
- Keep in mind that an especially talkative participant can crowd out others, and these others might eventually tune out if they don't see a role for themselves in the conversation. One of the best ways a facilitator can maintain the health of the conversation is by encouraging a wider range of participants. Depending on the setting and your own

comfort level, you might ask the room if anyone who hasn't spoken has something to say, or you can use subtler cues, like eye contact, to solicit contributions from participants who appear to be actively following the discussion but are not speaking. You might also generally encourage participants by saying something like: "If you're usually quiet, try to speak; if you're usually talkative, try taking a back seat."

- Encourage participants to respond to each other's points, and model that yourself by drawing on their comments and referring to them by name ("What X said got me thinking . . ."). The overall spirit should be a conversation where the group builds something together, rather than a debate where one side wins or loses. When it's necessary to disagree, make sure to keep it respectful by disagreeing with ideas rather than people.

- Linger on the questions and topics that seem to resonate, rather than constantly jumping around or forging ahead. ("Covering everything" is not necessarily important.)

Guiding Participants to a Great Discussion

Being a discussion facilitator requires a delicate balance: it's easy to fall into doing either too much or too little, especially with a bibliotherapy focus. On the one hand, the participants should ideally be the ones driving the conversation, and a facilitator who's taking up too much airtime might crowd out their voices. On the other hand, a facilitator can't simply sit back and let participants do all the work; part of your role is to provide the ground rules for the discussion and, if necessary, to gently apply those rules. Otherwise, a discussion can wind up dominated by a few loud voices, or (worst of all) go completely silent.

Think of a discussion like planting a garden. Most of the work comes at the beginning—ensuring that the ground is fertile, carefully planting and spacing your seeds, maybe even building a lattice to guide your plants in the right direction. This is to ensure that all your plants have the room and the conditions they need to grow. The plants that can spread and fill space most quickly could run roughshod over the others, and that's not good for the health of the garden. In the same way, when a discussion is set up and maintained in a fully hands-off way, the conditions are such that only some participants are likely to thrive—the ones who are most confident about jumping in—and the discussion as a whole can wind up going fallow. By contrast, if you lay the groundwork at the beginning for a discussion in which everyone feels comfortable speaking, then you're more likely to be able to sit back and watch the conversation blossom later on (though you may still have to gently "prune" those moments when someone is taking up too much of the sunlight!).

General Instructions to Readers before a Session

Depending on the group, it's quite likely that many participants will not have had a formal discussion about literature since high school or college. This can have a distorting effect on the conversation. Some participants may feel pressured to come up with "the right answer," or the "point" of the reading, which can effectively short-circuit the discussion. Others may fall silent because they don't know what they're supposed to say or where they should start.

Instead of approaching the meeting like a formal classroom discussion, encourage participants to think of it as similar to walking out of a theater with friends or family who've just watched the same movie. How might you start the conversation?

- You might ask a question about a part that confused you to see if everyone else was just as confused.
- You might talk about a favorite scene or a character whose motivations seemed interesting (or unconvincing).
- You might just talk about how the movie made you feel and see if it made other people feel the same way.

The point is that it's a conversation without a particular goal in mind. You just respond to other people's experience while sharing your own and see where it takes you!

DISCUSSION ICEBREAKERS

A discussion starts with noticing:

- "I found it hard to be sure why X acts this way."
- "This story jumps around in time a lot."
- "This seems like a weird metaphor for the poet to use."
- "Y seems like a really important moment here."
- "Why does the poet use a strict meter in this poem?"

Each of these conversation starters is an implicit opportunity for a further question: How does the text do this, or why?

Troubleshooting: Avoiding and Reacting to Participant Distress or Conflict

You may have been bracing yourself for this possibility while reading this chapter: Given that bibliotherapy can involve discussions of sensitive and difficult topics, what happens if participants become visibly distressed or come into conflict with each other?

In our experience, this happens rarely—less often than you might fear it would in a bibliotherapy setting. If you've advertised your group or event in a way that makes the content clear, participants will be prepared and are opting in for the topics that might come up. And an advantage of bibliotherapy is that while the topics may be personal, the medium of the text provides some distance from raw nerves. Nonetheless, because distress and conflict are some of the most stressful things that could happen and are likely a source of anxiety, it's a good idea to think about how to respond ahead of time.

Nobody enjoys distress or conflict, and unless you have professional experience with support groups or conflict mediation, you should not "steer into the skid" and approach these volatile situations head-on. But it's also important not to avoid potentially uncomfortable topics altogether; after all, that's what bibliotherapy is for! So how can you minimize the possibility of distress and conflict, and prevent it from derailing your session if it does arise, while still talking about the things that matter?

Prevention: Before the Session

- Select readings with your group and potential "trouble spots" related to your bibliotherapy topics in the broadest sense in mind. For example, does this reading contain slurs that would be offensive if repeated by a participant? If so, consider setting some ground rules about how to quote from the text.
- Avoid discussion questions that invite deeply held moral disagreements or ask participants to come down for or against a position. For example, instead of "Do you think [character X] did the right thing?" you might ask, "Why do you think [character X] might have acted this way?"
- Be clear in your marketing and prediscussion materials about what participants can expect. People are most likely to be hurt or defensive if they feel blindsided.

Redirection: During the Session

Your choices during the session when the discussion threatens to go off the rails range from gentle to forceful redirection. Here are some possibilities, which you might see as an escalating flowchart:

- If the discussion is starting to veer into personal or volatile territory, you can refer back to another topic or a more specific moment in the text: "That's an interesting connection, and I think that's a good segue to . . ." The idea here is to make the participant feel heard while moving things back onto safer ground.
- You can make that redirection explicit: "I really appreciate what you're sharing, but I want to make sure we [talk about X] / [keep the discussion focused on the text]."
- If a back-and-forth conflict has begun: "I don't think we're going to resolve this issue today, so let's move on to talk about X . . ."
- If someone says something offensive: "I'd ask that we not use that language here"; "Let's try not to generalize about groups of people here"; and so on. The tenor of your response will depend on the severity of the offense and whether it seems intended to provoke, and there are ways to respond and challenge without raising the temperate. A short and calm response is generally best. You can be gentle but firm,

suggesting that this is not up for debate. Keep in mind that for a very offensive comment or deliberate provocation, not responding is itself a response: your other participants are looking to you to establish a boundary, and if you don't address it, others will be more likely to either challenge the offending party directly or check out of the discussion.

- If a conflict becomes heated or personal: "I appreciate what an important issue this is, but I ask that we all keep this conversation friendly and disagree with ideas rather than people."

- If someone is quietly distressed, you can redirect the conversation without putting them on the spot—subtly if possible, more forcefully if necessary.

- If a speaker is in distress, make sure they feel validated: "I'm so sorry," "That sounds so difficult." You don't, however, want to derail the discussion and make it about one person. This can be handled gently: "I know this can be a really sensitive and personal issue, so maybe we can switch gears to talking about X."

- If someone is very distressed (crying, for instance), don't be afraid to break the flow of discussion to check in on them. "Hey, are you feeling okay, or do you need a minute?" "It's okay if you feel like you want to step out for a minute." "This sounds like a very personal and painful topic—we can move on as a group to something else if you'd like." Offer tissues if someone is crying but be careful about offering physical reassurance like a hug or taking someone's hand: they might not want to be touched.

- If all else fails, you can call for a short break or adjourn the discussion for the day.

In a Nutshell

Given their delicate balance, discussions will make or break your biblio-therapy-related program. Moderating a discussion is a skill that comes in handy in any work environment, whether the moderator is in charge or not. As a librarian running the session, are you fully in charge? Yes and no. Selecting an appropriate text that fulfills the purpose of the discussion has definitely put you in the captain's seat. However, as we all know from experience, discussions can take unexpected, exciting, and sometimes even dangerous turns, ending up in murky waters that are hard to navigate. Only a thorough preparation process, outlined in this chapter, can safeguard you and prevent the text (or, say, an eager participant) from taking over the wheel. You want to remain the one steering, even if you may need to adjust the course of your flagship program once in a while with the help of what you read in this chapter.

NOTE

1. W. H. Auden, *Making, Knowing, and Judging* (Oxford: Clarendon, 1960), 23, https://archive.org/details/makingknowingjud0000aude/page/22/mode/2up?view=theater.

08 | Hosting a Large Event

After conquering all the planning and preparation outlined in the previous chapters, perhaps you're looking for a new challenge: a large live event. Many of the steps toward a successful event are identical no matter what the type of library program, but the sensitive topics and focus on readers' emotional experience that come with bibliotherapy put extra pressure on some elements of the planning process and may even add a new wrinkle or two. To take the guesswork out of hosting a marquee event, this chapter shares best practices for putting together gatherings such as invited readings and moderated discussions, including how to craft a "playbook" that can keep the entire team on script and can avert disaster by providing solutions ahead of time for last-minute problems.

Running a Large Live Event (and Why You Want to Do It)

A marquee event with an invited author can build excitement for library programs and attract new participants. A bibliotherapy-inspired program may start with looking into inviting authors whose works are related to the most current mental health or community issues or, if you use contemporary literature as we do, the author of one of the texts that worked really well in your groups. Starting a program with a "big bang" is also a great marketing trick, but a large event open to the public requires special preparations and skills that can be acquired only by doing it. Hint: start small! Instead of inviting a big national name right away, explore local, lesser-known authors

> ### AT A GLANCE
>
> - Running a Large Live Event (and Why You Want to Do It)
> - Choosing a Guest Author
> - Creating Checklists and an Event Playbook
> - Engaging the Reader during Large Events

first. Moreover, practice your organization process and interview skills in a nonthreatening, nonchallenging environment such as in your book club, where the moderator role will come with similar challenges.

Nonetheless, in our experience, nothing can prepare you completely for the actual large event, or at least not to the point where you won't be second-guessing yourself: Why am I doing this? What was I thinking? Feeling that it seemed like a good idea but isn't any more is completely natural. It's a big undertaking—nerves are a sign that you're approaching the event with the appropriate seriousness!

The good news is that you can arrive 95 percent well prepared on the day of the event if you do your homework in terms of background preparation as mentioned in the previous section, as well as follow your checklist (see table 8.1). Mishaps will occur; but you will feel empowered to handle them, and participants will remember how great the event was rather than dwelling on how someone missed a beat.

Choosing a Guest Author

Once you have made your decision about hosting a large public event, the research part can begin with listing a couple of options for possible authors to invite, guided by your original bibliotherapy-related concepts, practices, and recent experiences. For any given topic or group, there are many possibilities. However, your audience—and budget—will quickly narrow down the list as you search for someone whose work speaks to the interests and concerns you've found in your library community. A short list of three to five is a manageable number for serious consideration. Once you feel comfortable with a few names based on your search (which can be surprisingly time consuming, we must warn you!), you can run the names by your partners and funding sources, providing a neatly organized background page on each.

Finding two or three authors available within your timeframe is the first step and probably plays just as much of a role in your decision as their fees (which can be quite shocking). Accomplished authors usually list their agent, manager, or publisher on their webpage as a contact. The scheduling part can be rather lengthy, so you may want to consider starting the process as soon as possible—four to six months before the event is a bare minimum, and earlier is better. A few other factors likely to play a role in your choice are:

- *Content.* The format of a guest speaker event is up to you, but having them read from their work is always a crowd-pleaser. It's helpful to have an idea for a text in mind before approaching the author. A passage that has gone over well in a smaller bibliotherapy-inspired group, or one that frames the issues you want to talk about in your interview or Q&A, is always a good bet. Whatever you decide, you'll just want to be sure that you've chosen something that will, in fact, please your crowd (see below) and is appropriate for your library setting.
- *Audience.* The author should be interesting and relevant to your target audiences, although you can be a bit broader in focus than with your book selections—a large event is a good opportunity to bring in new audiences for future programs! A bibliotherapeutic focus on specific topics and concerns allows you to attract those who might not come to a generic "author event," or who might not even have read the author in question but are intrigued by the topic.
- *Scheduling.* If you have hosted events before, you know that popular authors can get booked quickly, so try to schedule your event early.
- *Honorarium.* The range of fees that authors can charge was one of the surprises for us. Do your homework and make sure to specify ahead of time exactly what everyone is agreeing to—for instance, "a 60-minute reading and interview, recorded but not made available to the general public, with a 15-minute sound check before the event." Be aware that this and other parts of the contract may be subject to more-legal wrangling, even if it's just on the author's end of things.
- *Moderator.* Unless you are filling this role, you'll need to find and schedule one at the same time.

What really worked for us was reviewing all our resources and writing up a pros-and-cons list for each possible guest. The particular bibliotherapeutic topic of interest was already clear from the short-list stage, but watching authors speak at previous events or interviews (often available in whole or in part online) helped us get a feel for their suitability in a particular setting. The ideal speaker for a bibliotherapy-based event is an approachable, dynamic speaker who is willing to answer tricky questions (and even to be vulnerable), and who can convey their insights in a sympathetic and tactful manner when dealing with difficult subjects. In our experience, authors with college teaching experience are excellent performers in these events, picking up cues fast and answering questions in detail. It's okay to have a laconic guest speaker once in a while, and that's a possibility one has to prepare for, making sure to have more questions or different questions at hand.

Creating Checklists and an Event Playbook

Call us overly detail oriented, but we love templates, checklists, and scripts! A checklist-type template served as the foundation for many of our events. On the day of the event, a comprehensive "playbook," with dates, times, tactics, and methods all on a page or two, has helped us out during some difficult situations.

One Week Out

One week before the event, you may want to double-check that your reading materials are all available for your readers, the guest speaker, and the moderator, including the text to be presented by the guest speaker (especially if you wish to drop a link in the chat to an online version so the audience can follow along). Checking in with the author, moderator, and IT support at this time will get everyone on the same page and allow any potential issues to be addressed before they escalate. For example, you haven't received enough registrations. If you haven't already done so, check your registration link for errors such as dead links or wrong mandatory fields.

In your playbook, this is the time to finalize all the names and correct titles for all the people listed on your thank-you list and to plan for potential mishaps and how to remediate them. This is also a good time to confirm your contingency plans for any technical or other snafus! At one event, a videoconferencing technical issue almost left us without a guest; thanks to prior planning, we were able to guide the author through the process of phoning in to the meeting.

TABLE 8.1

Event Checklist: One Week before the Event

	TASK	NOTES
1 week before	Check if reading material is available (print/online)	Check access issues, such as number of physical copies, user licenses
	Send in a mock registration to find dead links, wrong mandatory fields, and other errors	
	Check if moderator is ready	Finalize discussion sheets; send and post printouts, if needed
	Check if guest speaker/author is ready	Ensure access; check help with IT Send sample questions
	Have playbook ready	Plan for failure (tech mishaps, guest or staff no-shows)
	Check in with tech support Set up access	Communicate needs clearly; test technology
	Collect and/or confirm names/ titles of anyone who has helped.	Double-check spelling and/or pronunciation, even for "obvious" or "easy" names
	Post about event on social media Write teaser blog post Send out reminders with link	Keep audience in mind for content, style, frequency, and timing

On the Day of the Event: One Hour Before

Whether it's an event in the library or remotely, you may want to show up at least an hour before everyone else. Particularly for an online event, the sound check and other tests of your equipment will need to happen with enough time remaining to fix any issues. For an online event, this also means confirming that your guest and moderator can log in. (If the guest is available before the day of the event, do consider checking at least a week beforehand whether or not they can log in. This avoids any surprises. But sometimes guests won't be able to commit to tasks long before the event.)

This is the time to make last-minute changes to the playbook if necessary. We also usually agree on some kind of a mayday signal before an event and how to send it (private chat, text message, or maybe using a code phrase—for partners who know each other well, eye contact or a certain tone of voice may be enough to communicate distress!). Boilerplate signal words are also great cues to indicate transitions, which are necessary, even if we like to minimize going back and forth.

TABLE 8.2

Event Checklist: Day of the Event

TIMING	TASK	NOTES
1 hr. before	Room is ready OR Zoom works Designate a cohost if online	Double-check schedule; run software updates
	Technology: sound check with moderator, guest, and panelists	Review backup plan and adjust if needed
	Have playbook ready	Make minor adjustments if needed
	Agree on transitions and how to signal problems (e.g., text backchannel)	Limit switching back and forth between presenters, time lost in transitions
15 min. before	Open doors OR Zoom room	Remember that it's already showtime!
5 min. before	Make first welcome announcement ("The event will start soon.")	If online: both via speaker and chat

You should have posted or provided a schedule, clear to all participants, that designates when the doors will open or when the online participants can start joining. Some conferencing applications use different labels, such as panelists for the speakers and guests for the participants. Make sure you're clear on these labels if they affect how you communicate with or about the author, your staff, and participants. Remember, anyone will be able to see and hear you as soon as they enter, even if you don't notice them!

We like to give orientation announcements first, to make sure that people are in the right place, and then a technical announcement that explains if and how participants can interact with the presenters. The decision is all yours. For really large public events, we tend to disable both chat and Q&A and opt for incorporating prescreened questions that the audience submitted upon registration. A small event with local participants who are familiar with each other, or where the goal is to bring them closer by discussing sensitive, bibliotherapy-worthy topics, may offer more interactions, but the hosts have to be prepared how to handle impromptu questions. We had no problem using the "raise hand" method online and in the library too. Others opt for a keyword in the chat, such as *STACK*, and the moderator will call on the person next in line.

Any event should start with a welcome and introductions that include a short bio of the author with their major accomplishments. Your background research will come in handy here again. If there's any more housekeeping or ground rules to mention (other than the ones in the pre-event announcement), those should go here.

We like to start with the author reading their own text early to set the tone. The selection, in agreement with the author, can be an unpublished or recently published text that wouldn't take more than ten minutes to read and fits into your bibliotherapy program. You may want to time it yourself before the event to see how it goes, at a range of comfortable reading paces.

An experienced moderator can take over from here, running the discussion as scheduled or with minor adjustments to the context. In an author interview scenario, the event should look like two old friends talking about books, even if they just met the morning of! Whether or not the participants are invited to chime in, it's advisable to prepare with some easy warm-up questions related to the text the author has just read from. Follow-up questions should hew to the original plan, even if they're asked in a different order.

The five- and ten-minute warnings for the end of the event are important points for the moderator to be aware of. Even if your event is going really well, at this point you may want to ask a final question, such as "Is there a question that you haven't been asked today but would like to answer?" Some guests might offer to overstay a bit, but remember that you don't want to abuse their generosity (or your audience's patience . . .).

Have your closing remarks ready five minutes before ending. Make sure, too, that the person responsible for extending gratitude to the author and all others has enough time to do so, listing the names and roles of everyone who contributed to your event's success. A small token of appreciation, such as a handwritten thank-you, will go a long way toward preserving their goodwill for your next event. Remember to thank the audience too! It shouldn't take longer than two or three minutes, especially if you have everything spelled out in your event playbook.

TABLE 8.3

Event Checklist: During the Event

TIMING	TASK	NOTES
At start	Make second welcome announcement	If online: both via speaker and chat
	Hit RECORD if to be recorded	Do not use autorecord
	Introduce yourself, speakers, and guests	Scripting this part in your playbook will take away the jitters
	Establish ground rules	Use same rules throughout all events
5 min. into event	Moderator/guest: Read text out aloud (whole or excerpt)	Do not ask participants to do this, even if they've read the text before. Limit reading to 5–10 min. If chosen text is short: read all If long: use excerpt
10–15 min. into event	Start discussion with a warm-up (nonthreatening) question	Have conversation starters at hand Tailor them to your audience
	Follow with questions (6–10) as needed Change planned order if necessary	Going off on tangents: have language for how to get back on topic
	Encourage everyone to speak up (if it's an open discussion) Help them respond to each other Let the discussion flow	Not all participants are interested in all questions. Some might take up too much conversation space—prepare ways to redirect the discussion.
10 min. before end	Ask final question, announcing it as last one	Close discussion, even if going well Have a concluding prompt at hand
2–3 min. before end	Wrap it up by thanking guests, participants, assistants by name	Read out correct names/titles from your playbook
At end	In person: Make sure participants leave in an orderly manner Online: Turn off recording, if applicable In person or online: Save recording in the cloud	In person: Have a plan to put an end to conversations, such as pointing out a related display

After the Event

Whether online or in person, although you've thanked everyone in public, it won't hurt repeating the thank-you routine after the recording has been turned off and all the guests have left. (If participants fail to take the hint, leave the physical or virtual space yourselves and reconvene somewhere more private; above all, make sure the author has an "exit ramp" at the designated end time if they choose to take it!)

In our experience, this is also the best time to recap and evaluate what went well and what could have been done better. Having everything fresh in all contributors' minds is a great opportunity to grow—you don't want to miss it! In fact, our favorite part of the post-event checklist is the event recap and immediate reflections. There's no more sincere assessment than right after an event, when every single little issue still looks magnified.

We also recommend setting up a timeline-type of template for the following hours, days, and weeks to make sure that all thank-you letters are sent, the guest and moderator are paid, post-event recap is posted on social media with pictures, and if permitted, the recording or any other content is shared. Sending out official thank-you letters can wait until the next day, but if you've planned ahead, at this point you can just hit send and get it done with your letters already typed up.

You'll also be busy sharing the event recap on social media and your website over the next few days. We like posting something short with a picture the next day after the event and a longer blog post within a week, providing a great opportunity to promote the entire program, the next event, and, ultimately, the library.

TABLE 8.4

Event Checklist: After the Event

TIMING	TASK	NOTES
Immediately	Stay until everyone leaves Thank staff and discuss what went well	Best time to recap and evaluate—don't miss it!
Next hours	Send out official thank-you letters if applicable	Draft before, personalize after event
Next day	Post event recap and photos on social media Write teaser blog post about next event	This should be in keeping with previous marketing strategy (i.e., based on your target audience)
Next week	Blog about the event Share content if applicable	Post one or multiple perspectives Obtain permissions

Engaging the Reader during Large Events

With the audience allowed to participate, you may want to encourage everyone to speak up, but you have to accept that not everyone wants to. It takes a while to learn how to let a discussion take its own course and flow naturally, for the moderator and participants both; but with some scaffolding, a few comments here and there, it's not that difficult to keep track of the threads and help participants respond to each other.

It's virtually impossible to run a meaningful discussion in large groups, especially online. For these occasions, we came up with the idea of tacking an extra field to the registration form: "What would you like to ask the author?" We then collected all the questions submitted for each and every event in a spreadsheet. The convenience of incorporating representative questions into the interview-type discussion not only justified our decision right away but also showed some patterns of what our event registrants are usually interested in. With this method, you can be sure to cover the topics of widest interest without the unwieldiness of calling on people in an enormous virtual room and exposing yourselves to technical problems.

WORKING WITH QUESTIONS FROM PARTICIPANTS

Other than the recurring questions that come up at every author event, here are a few bibliotherapy-focused ones from participants of our events.

- As a writer who delves into hard topics, what self-care do you do?
- Do you have to prepare yourself to write about painful things? And do you do any self-care to release any emotions after writing about difficult subjects?
- How do you know when you have lived with a topic or issue long enough to write about it?
- What gives you hope?
- Can you say something about how to have balance in self-expression—giving voice to your personal experience while maintaining ownership over it?

Before Going Off the Rails

Excused or not, it's inevitable that the conversation will start to digress. Not every digression is a disaster; you might wind up in interesting and unexpected territory! The role of the moderator is to keep things running smoothly, and sometimes that means being open to improvisation, letting some segments run longer or shorter in order to maintain interest and a sense of organic flow. But if you feel the conversation start to get sidetracked or head in an uncomfortable direction, the best course is to smoothly redirect the conversation back on track. As long as you don't seem flustered, the audience is likely either to not notice or to admire your command of the situation. Preparing some language or strategies will be helpful.

SAMPLE LANGUAGE TO SAVE THE DAY

Here are a few ideas to get back on track without escalating the situation at a larger, public event when the moderator has the difficult task of gently guiding the guest back to the question at hand or silencing a member of the audience.

Simple and Neutral
- That's fascinating! It reminds me of . . . (*Segue back to planned topic.*)
- Actually, one of the questions we received also asks . . . (*Pull out a related question.*)

Time-Based
- What a fascinating idea! I wish we had more time to explore it, but unfortunately . . .
- That's such an interesting topic—I'm sure we could dedicate a whole session to that!

De-escalating an Audience Question (Going On Long or Becoming Confrontational)
- Thanks for your [question/comment]—I want to give our guest a chance to respond . . .
- (*If a back-and-forth becomes heated or stagnant:*) This is an interesting line of conversation, but I'll have to ask that we move on so we can get to all the topics we hope to address today.

In a Nutshell

This chapter offered practical guidelines and ideas to consider when planning your own large event, defining best practices and basic principles. Librarians are not only familiar with how to do the research needed before setting up a program, but they excel at it. Use this skill to your advantage and make informed decisions in advance. Any live event, whether a small-group discussion or a large author event, will be unpredictable and sometimes challenging. But with clear expectations and legwork ahead of time, you can achieve the confidence described by the poet Maya Angelou: "Hoping for the best, prepared for the worst, and unsurprised by anything in between."[1]

NOTE

1. Maya Angelou, *I Know Why the Caged Bird Sings* (1963; New York: Random House, 2009), 283.

PART IV

Turning Outward

09 | Traditional Marketing

When it comes to marketing your bibliotherapy-inspired program, you may simply want to stick with what has already worked for promoting your other programs in the library. If you are confident in your marketing experience, feel free to skim when we're telling you what you already know. However, if you need a bit more guidance or need confirmation that you're on the right track, keep reading! This chapter will help you understand the intricacies of event marketing in a library from budgets to social capital, with a particular eye toward bibliotherapy. Investing in content development for marketing purposes in an early phase might seem counterintuitive, but frontloading this part of the project is worth the time in the long run. In addition to realistic, up-front planning that considers people—users and staff alike—as a top priority, the marketing strategies suggested here (and which harken back to chapter 3) are straightforward and honest: what you see is what you get.

Set Your Vision

The concept behind your bibliotherapy-inspired program will define your marketing strategies. You want your program to reach the audiences it was designed for and for those audiences to have a clear, accurate, appealing idea of what your program will do. Carefully selected marketing tools can help you reach the right audiences, get their attention, and communicate with them effectively.

The central consideration here is creating what marketers call a *brand identity*: a sense of who you

AT A GLANCE

- Set Your Vision
- Follow the $$$
- Work with What You Have
- Know Thy Users
- Get Buy-In (aka Try Participatory Design)
- Build on Your Approval
- Time Your Launch
- Get Feedback
- Create Synergies

are and what you're about that you can impart to prospective clients. Think of your brand as a potpourri of everything that defines your program: from the distinctive features of your program and the benefits it promises down to aesthetic details like writing style, color palette, font, graphic themes, and so on.

For a bibliotherapy-inspired reading program, there are some basic considerations for determining your marketing decisions. For instance, how central is therapeutic reading to your program's identity? (If it's a main focus for the program, it should be prominent in marketing!) What kind of readers do we hope to attract? (If you're marketing to seniors, youth-oriented platforms like TikTok are probably a poor use of time!) Does our reading material skew toward difficult or painful topics? (If so, a marketing tone that would sound fun for another program might come across as flippant here.) Developing and implementing your brand can't happen without a clear vision—but you may also find that articulating your brand forces you to better define and streamline that vision, creating a stronger sense of the program's identity for yourselves as well as your prospective participants.

Follow the $$$

Planning for your project includes looking into your library's budget, as discussed in chapter 3. Once you get the green light, you can start breaking down the program budget into its components. For marketing, you may not even need a humongous amount, if you can apply or adapt some of the ideas in this chapter to your setting.

One idea is to piggyback on a well-established program such as summer reading or holiday preparations. You can adopt existing and successful marketing tools right away or repurpose them to your new vision. For example, back in the day, we started reading short stories with just a few students on campus and marketed the program in a cost-conscious manner that one might even call frugal or penny-pinching. It took us several years to end up running Summer Tales, a three-month, campuswide reading initiative during the pandemic with a budget large enough to invite accomplished authors.

THE INCOMPLETE LIST OF MARKETING TOOLS

The list of tools to market your bibliotherapy-focused program is endless and constantly evolving. By "marketing tool," we mean a communication channel used to reach your audience. You may want to choose more than one from this list to deliver your message. Note that your choice of preferred medium should be tailored to your topic and the audience you want to attract—different tools will reach different groups!

- Signs, flyers, cards, postcards, bookmarks, and door hangers work fine as long as they feature carefully crafted language and graphics matching your bibliotherapy focus.
- Brochures and posters can provide in-depth orientation for those on the verge of joining. Remember to place them visibly but with an option for your users to pick them up inconspicuously.
- Buttons and coloring sheets are great conversation starters and will actively engage your potential audience if offered at an open-house event.
- Window displays, display cases, and ad hoc exhibits have the biggest appeal as passive programming methods. Bibliotherapy-themed displays will attract shy readers discreetly but effectively.
- Announcements, email blasts, media releases, newsletter articles, websites, and public speeches are all great traditional tools. Focusing on wellness in general or on a pressing issue in the community, these can double as marketing tools for your bibliotherapy-themed program.

Work with What You Have

For marketing purposes, first you may want to find out about your available assets—not only the titles in your collection, but your human resources too. Working with what you already have and people whose skills you already trust will give you a sense of security in marketing a program with sensitive topics.

You can also mobilize your social capital and share marketing with any other program, unit, or organization in your community. As a happy accident, we often discovered mutually rewarding partnerships within the university and beyond. For instance, a social media partner from the School of Environmental and Biological Sciences that our library serves turned out to be a professional photographer very much interested in guided reading for mental health. Bringing her talents to our events gave her a lot of content to post to the school's official social media channels and gave us outstanding photo documentation—a textbook case of a win-win situation.

Know Thy Users

In this book, chapter 5 discusses the importance of a thorough knowledge of your library users' demographics before you start developing a biblio-therapy-inspired program. The same level of familiarity with your potential audience is a must for marketing too. If you're familiar with your users' needs and interests, it seems almost self-explanatory to harness your marketing, media, and communications strategies to develop your message and select the best tools to connect with your target audiences. Keep in mind your secondary audiences too—that is, the people you'd like to see in your library.

Once you've figured out how to match your program with your users, your marketing strategy should be a no-brainer. Using two previous examples, for your retirees who come over to the library every Friday as a group, a short face-to-face introduction of the program is likely to bring the best results, or at least can gauge interest. On the contrary, targeting high school or teenage users is different, even if they routinely stop by at the library on their way home. They may expect to be reached via social media, especially if the library has already established a connection with them on their preferred social media platforms.

READ MORE ON MARKETING IN LIBRARIES

1. *The Librarian's Nitty-Gritty Guide to Social Media* by Laura Solomon
2. *Marketing Plans in Action: A Step-by-Step Guide for Libraries, Archives, and Cultural Organizations* by Amanda L. Goodman
3. *Marketing with Social Media: A LITA Guide* by Beth Thomsett-Scott

Get Buy-In (aka Try Participatory Design)

You may want to pick the brains of others to ensure that your program will be beneficial to your participants, rather than trying to impose your own vision. *Participatory design* is the term for this kind of crowdsourcing, and it provides some significant advantages for bibliotherapy projects too. Your participants are an untapped source of creativity who can provide insights about what appeals to people like themselves—and further, there's nothing like a sense of ownership to get people excited about a program.

Techniques such as brainstorming, mind mapping, whiteboarding, setting up surveys or focus groups, or just plain one-on-one dialogs will take you closer to fruition while planning your marketing campaign. Having to communicate your initial idea to diverse audiences through various channels will demand that you look at the original idea from different angles and tailor your pitch accordingly.

Developing Your Pitch

To create a compelling message to be included in all your marketing material, you may want to focus on the following three points. You may not need all of them in all communications, and the order might need to be adjusted to your audience and the type of marketing material.

- *What you do.* Explain your program in simple language targeting your audience.
- *Why you do it.* Reveal the community's need and the benefits of your program.
- *How you do it.* Establish your authority, quote testimonials, link to feedback.

Build on Your Approval

Developing your marketing strategies begins with the project proposal, long before getting approved by the administration, as you write your proposal with the sensitive nature of bibliotherapy-worthy topics in mind. Once the project is approved, the text from your proposal is ready to assume its various formats and embark on its marketing journey. Whether making it short for social media or letting yourself go a bit more verbose on the website and in a blog, now is the time to break out the fancy fonts and appealing formatting to adjust the content to your theme, program, and marketing tool. With the help of your creative allies, images and slogans used in the proposal can be turned into a whole branding kit.

Time Your Launch

As an integral part of the marketing strategies, planning, staging, and scheduling the rollout of a program or single event should always include a distinct marketing timeline: the how, when, and where of all promotional activities. Some librarians like using sophisticated project-management software applications to map these; however, a shared spreadsheet or even a plain whiteboard with some moveable magnets will do too.

With the project approved, it's a good idea to plan out several updates for your audience across various platforms. If you have a blog or library website, you can post updates there and link to them on various social media. Plan early and wisely, and your success is inevitable.

MARKETING IDEAS

Setting Up Your Timeline

Whether you promote your program via traditional channels or social media, it may help to establish a progressive timeline, similar to what worked for us below. Note the lack of any reference to therapy or bibliotherapy in our examples. It depends on your goals and audience if you opt for pushing the wellness or therapy angle. In our case, the selected reading material did the work for us.

Start with a Teaser (Required)
A poster placed outside and inside the library at the beginning of the fall semester in 2019 served as a teaser and hold-the-date for our semester-long reading program with the following text, while a QR code pointed to the website with more information.

Join us as often as you like to read for fun in the fall semester. We'll be reading short fiction and talking about it together— That's it! It's like SPEED-DATING THE LIBRARY STACKS.

Follow Up with an Invitation (Required)
Next, participants were invited by posters (print and online), as well as with an email blast using the same language and some more details, such as options and prompts to register, along with some encouragement, targeting the audience, college students in a science library.

Sign Up for Our Fall 2019 Sessions!

Join us as often as you like as we read short fiction for fun in the fall semester. We will be reading short fiction and talking about it together—that's it! It's like SPEED-DATING THE LIBRARY STACKS. You'll encounter writers from classic to contemporary, discuss the experience with friends, and maybe even start a fling with a new favorite author or genre.
No expertise needed—No assignments or quizzes—No commitment to making every meeting.

Send Out an Event Recap to Engage the Ones on the Verge (Optional)

If you hosted a successful kickoff event, you have all the reason to sing your own praises for a noble cause: talk those undecided potential participants into giving the program a try. After the recap, you can use the language from your background research, as we did, then repeat the details of registration from the invitation.

> Tales We Read was kicked off with a sprint and flash! It's not too late to join us!
>
> *In the first session we are reading and discussing the short story "Eight Bites" by Carmen Maria Machado. In "Eight Bites," Machado goes inside the mind of a woman who undergoes bariatric weight loss surgery. It's often said that food is family, and the relationship of Machado's narrator to food and her own body is refracted through her relationships with the women of her family: an iron-willed mother, gossipy sisters, and a concerned daughter. Weaving realistic storytelling with a surrealist twist, Machado explores the complicated feelings around a simple clinical procedure: desire, shame, love, envy, and a sense of having "lost" something more than merely weight.*

Post the Schedule as a Reminder (Optional)

Unless you want to close your group to new participants after the first session, you should keep up the marketing even once it's begun. And even then, you might want to promote the next iteration of the program by reminding people of the one currently running.

> A new discussion starts every other Wednesday! Check out our public guide for related information and more fun reading ideas.

Keep Up the Interest with News Items (Optional)

Thinking forward, you can reach out to your current and prospective participants with additional material to read and reflect, such as worksheets you post online or make available in the library as promotion for your next program.

New resources are available to download!

Colson Whitehead, Lydia Davis, and Carmen Maria Machado are among the most exciting writers in contemporary fiction, and we have discussion guides available for three of their short stories. From Whitehead's playful metaphor of dating as a movie, to Davis's flash fiction about intimacy and fantasy, to Machado's haunting tale of a woman's relationship to her body and her family as she undergoes weight-loss surgery, these stories spark conversation and linger in the mind long after they're put down. See the sheets for Whitehead's "Down in Front," Davis's "Betrayal," and Machado's "Eight Bites" on the "Discussion Material" page.

Get Feedback

How did you do? Feedback also contributes to a solid marketing strategy. Program participants are used to being invited to submit feedback. Moreover, many will share their thoughts whether you want it or not, in person or on social media. Learn how to turn that to your advantage!

In addition to collecting feedback on social media, qualitative and quantitative, old-fashioned surveys can serve the same purpose—that is, to gauge interest, if any, or to solicit ideas to improve. A brave idea is to add a feedback box to your website or blog in a sidebar. (It's feasible only if you are absolutely sure that someone will constantly monitor submissions; a suggestion box that goes directly to the spam folder is worse than none at all.) The interactive nature of social media platforms makes soliciting feedback there easier but also riskier: you may get negative feedback or out-of-context comments that other users can see, and your posts will require constant monitoring to ensure that these comments don't go overlooked and unanswered.

As for tools, Qualtrics and LibWizard are excellent and intuitive, if your library is a subscriber. Among freebies, SurveyMonkey or Google Forms are easy to use and go a long way, and there are tons of outstanding online software applications to supplement them with. As for the content of your feedback solicitation, it really depends on what you want to know and need to know. It's nice to set up a survey instrument that allows for plenty of praise, but you will learn more from the questionnaires that dig a bit deeper and address uncertainties and pain points.

Create Synergies

Creating synergies is also a critical element in promoting a bibliotherapy-centered program. A simple but efficient way is resource sharing, such as combining marketing efforts with another program or organization, or reusing content, in a meaningful way, in different contexts. Table 9.1 illustrates the shift involved in reframing your existing program marketing for bibliotherapy-centered programming.

TABLE 9.1

Marketing for Traditional and Bibliotherapy-Centered Programs

	TRADITIONAL	BT-CENTERED
Marketing objective	For participants to use a resource or the collection	For participants to talk about and reflect on texts for individual therapeutic benefits
Target audience	Broad, diverse	Specific, theme driven
	Current library users	Potential/new users as well as current ones
Displays in-house	Anywhere, prominent	Safe place, respect privacy
Align branding primarily with	Library's mission	Target audience's need
Synergies	With other library programs	With community partners
		With activities for creativity and reflection
Feedback channel	Public	Anonymous

Each library has its own preferences and protocols to partner with organizations in their community with similar goals. Bibliotherapy-centered projects tend to bring people together in reflection, creativity, and setting priorities. It's worth a try to find new ones for your new project! It may pave the path to new partnerships, new synergies, and new horizons for the entire library.

In a Nutshell

Although each library setting is different, established and unorthodox ideas presented step by step in this chapter can be used to promote bibliotherapy initiatives across libraries, including yours. There is no single path to create and execute a successful marketing plan. Building on local talent, resources, and audiences presents a great opportunity for you to experiment with the methods listed here—from traditional in-house marketing strategies to unconventional forms of outreach and community partnerships—until you find that sweet spot. Remember, your marketing won't happen until you get started . . . dive right in as early as possible!

10 | Social Media Marketing

Facebook, X (formerly Twitter), YouTube, or Instagram? There is no one-size-fits-all answer. You have watched social media platforms come and go, generations flocking to new platforms and snubbing last year's favorites. If you're already a social media pro, feel free to skip or skim the portions of this chapter that deal with the basics of each platform. But if you're wondering how to incorporate social media into your marketing strategy for bibliotherapy-inspired programs, you've come to the right place! This chapter will help you make strategic decisions about which platforms to use and how, targeting your audience on the platforms they use and getting the message out in an efficient, platform-savvy, relatable yet professional way. Social media may seem like fun, but managing your library's presence is work, and this chapter will give you ideas for how to allocate your resources effectively and make that work count.

Your Social Media Accounts

Setting up an account on a social media platform is very easy—almost too easy! Sustainability is another question. To keep a social medial profile fresh, you will have to post quite frequently, preferably several times a week. You will also consume and, depending on the platform, repost peers' content and respond to followers quickly. Maintaining a high-quality and well-maintained blog, with weekly posts of 800 to 1,200 words, can be particularly time consuming if you want to create meaningful bibliotherapy-focused content.

AT A GLANCE

- Your Social Media Accounts
- Choosing Social Media Platforms
- X (formerly Twitter): The Tip of the Iceberg
- Instagram: A Picture Tells a Thousand Words
- Facebook: Instant Promotion
- Blogs: Your Authentic Voice
- Creating Synergies: Putting It All Together

Frequency is key; posting once a month is probably not enough to keep your hard-earned followers. Linking various accounts to automate cross-posting across platforms is a great shortcut and can help keep your social media presence consistent.

In general, libraries already use social media in a variety of ways, such as simply making their presence known, informing users about changes in library hours or closures, and promoting programs or resources. The easiest way is to tie your new accounts with a bibliotherapy focus to your library's established presence. A purposefully selected profile photo can represent your program well and can provide visual identity. Your "About" page should be original, introducing the program creatively in a brief elevator pitch, indicating your program's focus on therapeutic reading and specific topics of interest. Adding some keywords for SEO and singing your own praises are not only allowed but strongly encouraged!

The best part of all social media applications is that you can use them to funnel traffic to your website, blog posts, and programs related to bibliotherapy. Using the right social media strategies—such as posting links regularly pointing to your website or blog post—will not only get people talking, commenting, and liking, but will also drive traffic to the actual content, your program. This is exactly how you should focus your time and effort, rather than simply wanting to increase engagement metrics on the individual platforms.

Monitoring your social media accounts closely is a must, especially with potentially sensitive topics. It means either setting up alerts or checking the feeds religiously a few times a day. Negative comments (whether well-reasoned or not) and random spam do not come up often, but leaving them unaddressed can be detrimental to the reputation of your library—not necessarily the actual content, but the fact that no one bothered to respond to or delete them.

BEST BANG FOR YOUR BUCK

Librarians on a budget (is there any other kind?) are eager to find out where to get the best bang for their buck. Social media might mean additional tasks for everyone involved, but it's something that can be planned ahead of time, with scheduled posts, predesigned images, and opportunities to repackage content or work from a template, piggybacking your bibliotherapy-inspired programs on existing material and practices. The trick is to present who you are, remain relevant, and adjust the content to the needs of the program and the actual audience within the larger community, remaining mindful of your budgetary constraints. As intentionally bibliotherapy-inspired librarians, you are perfectly capable of making informed decisions on your content and how to communicate it to your audience.

User expectations of social media presence have grown incredibly—almost to a point where libraries are in a rather disadvantageous position because we as a culture have gotten used to a twenty-four-hour response time. It doesn't mean that libraries cannot benefit from social media even if they lack staffing similar to large chains or online retailers. Social media platforms—with their measurable data on impact indicators such as reach, views, impressions, and shares—serve as great quantitative assessment tools. Social media can also lead potential patrons to more substantial engagement with the library website or the library itself. And assessment can help you track how often your social media profile leads to such outcomes and how to improve it.

Choosing Social Media Platforms

Any social media network can help you build your online brand and increase overall visibility if you manage to develop meaningful connections with your users, current and potential. From the many available options, the platforms discussed here are perhaps the most popular choices, each representing a type of complementary social media strategy that benefits from cross-platform promotion. If you are hesitant to use social media for bibliotherapy projects or don't know where to start, start anywhere and take baby steps to establish a habit. It will get easier over time. Just give your program a chance to shine!

Social media platforms come with their own benefits. Short informational communications can take your reader to longer meaningful content, such as linking from a tweet to a thoughtful blog post. But these platforms come with hazards as well. A bibliotherapy-focused program, at a minimum, will probably touch upon sensitive topics. The concise nature of a post might come with some hidden pitfalls: the short space risks exposing each word choice to critique, missing important nuance; even the concision itself can come across as insensitive or flippant. It's not just text, either—images are not immune to social media's microscope effect! You'll want to be careful what you say when representing your program, and you may want to restrict the ability to post to team members who are similarly circumspect.

Additionally, planning your social media strategy should also include a checklist to avoid common mishaps, such as using the wrong hashtag, forgetting to tag an important collaborator, having incorrect or missing links to related content or cross-posts, or simply not fitting the style of the medium.

X (Formerly Twitter): The Tip of the Iceberg

As we write this, X (formerly Twitter) is still relevant but has an uncertain future. In any case, it has come a long way, from a punchline about modern attention spans to one of the premier places for up-to-the-minute news, reactions, and conversation. Mindful of X's potential and pitfalls, bibliotherapy-focused programming can take advantage of the platform's concise style and ease of linking to more substantial content. A tweet is ideal for teasing interesting details about an event, with a link to something more substantial such as a blog post or an item on your website. Keep in mind that the algorithm prioritizes recency, so a few frequent reminders ("We hope you're excited for our author talk next Tuesday! Details: [link]") rarely go amiss and may catch new viewers who missed the original announcement.

Instagram: A Picture Tells a Thousand Words

Instagram is probably the best platform for branding and engaging users, and it already has notably lively conversations about mental health and wellness (even if many of those conversations are about the platform's own hazards!). Instagram's emphasis on mobile access, ease of use, and appealing visuals attracts a large group of users, diverse in every metric. Given the platform's popularity across different generations, it's expected from a library or program to have some Instagram presence nowadays where users can follow, tag, share, and more, adding to user engagement.

To market your program successfully on Instagram, you'll want to start with the visual. The best photos are ones you've taken yourself, whether specifically for Instagram or repurposed; if you resort to images found online, you'll want to be sure about the copyright. Posting a photo of the cover of a book sitting on a table or, better yet, in your hands as you read it, is an easy and engaging visual. Although the main feature is the picture, preferably of high quality, it's worth experimenting with captions, tags, questions, or any other hook that captures the user's attention. The possibilities are endless—if you know your program and your audience. Think about including a call to some kind of engagement (a *call to action*, or CTA, in marketing), so as to prompt users to break away from scrolling and take some action like checking out a post, registering for an event, recommending a bibliotherapy-themed book, or going to the library to find something to read.

Facebook: Instant Promotion

The first wildly successful mainstream social media platform, Facebook is probably the largest and most recognized social media network that reaches the broadest audience worldwide. Rumors of its demise have been greatly exaggerated: some users may be abandoning it for newer sites, but for many, Facebook remains the primary social media platform. This alone should encourage any program director to focus energies on developing a strong Facebook presence. Facebook can easily (and serendipitously) connect you with a target audience interested in reading for mental health. Linked to your Instagram account, Facebook also saves time and creates a consistent voice for you on social media. The importance of a consistently inclusive and welcoming voice can't be stressed enough for your bibliotherapy-focused program.

Blogs: Your Authentic Voice

In marketing, blogs serve the same purpose as any other social media tool: they grab attention, connect you with your users, create visibility for your program, boost traffic to your website, and enhance the discoverability of your program or project. Writing meaningful posts with unique and original content will make your program stand out, your voice more authentic, and will cast you as an online authority in your niche bibliotherapy-related project.

While one person is usually enough to run any of the above-mentioned social media platforms (although you may want to have backups for each), an effective and well-maintained blog for a bibliotherapy-focused program needs a rotating cast of authors to ensure diversity in topic, style, format, and ultimately, reach. A decent blogger can write about almost any topic on short notice, and that's fine for certain content, such as announcing programs. But remarkable bloggers communicate their message better because they sound authentic and genuinely interested in their topics. Posts written by talented bloggers generate more interest, attract more people, and reach out to broader audiences, regardless of the assorted topic. The texts that make both the author and the audience happy (as demonstrated by page views and time spent on page) are usually the ones written on a topic the author is passionate about and that have a purpose, such as promoting a program, a guest author, or a favorite book.

EXAMPLE BLOG POST

"Carmen Maria Machado, between Persons"

A heads-up:
This post, like Machado's memoir, discusses intimate partner abuse.

There are two distinctive formal features of Carmen Maria Machado's *In The Dream House: A Memoir* that are apparent from early on. The first is that this memoir is fractured into a series of short forays, usually just one or two pages, that approach the central story of an abusive lesbian relationship from different angles while relating its course in roughly chronological order. Often these miniature chapters are named after different genres of narrative ("Dream House as Noir," "Dream House as Stoner Comedy"), as well as genres of space (e.g., "Dream House as Inner Sanctum") and mythic or folklore tropes ("Dream House as Bluebeard," "Dream House as River Lethe"). The collage of genres highlights how numbingly ubiquitous the abuse of women is to so many of our cultural stories, while also carving out space in the predominantly heterosexual imaginary of domestic violence for the relatively unacknowledged issue of abusive relationships between women. The experimentation with genre also incidentally shows off Machado's range as a writer, from experimental fiction and polemic essay to those under-respected kinds of writing that provoke a bodily response: suspense, erotica, horror.

Read the whole post in its entirety at sites.rutgers.edu/books-we-read/carmen-maria-machado-between-persons/.

Sample Blog Types

Blog posts provide endless opportunities to share information about a program or an event, spread the word, recap what happened, generate interest, recommend material, explain processes, and more. A few types you may want to consider setting up as templates are as follows.

- *Pure information sharing:* news, teasers, invitations, any repackaged content, "in case you missed it" posts. These are the easiest to write and have *just* enough information.
- *Scaffolding/propping:* reminders, recaps, schedules, and other gentle nudges. These depend largely on your community. You may want to develop your own style without sounding condescending. A reminder like "Don't forget to sign up" or "What are you waiting for?" can strike some as friendly, but others may not appreciate feeling pushed ("I was waiting to decide, thank you very much, and now I'm leaning no!").
- *Staff picks:* book reviews with a focus on individual titles, a single author, topic, or genre from the collection. With its potential to promote both your program and the collection, you definitely want to insert this type of post into the rotating blog schedule.
- *The personal touch (our favorite):* blog posts reviewing a book or reflecting on an event, a phenomenon, a genre, or anything else related to personal well-being. Such posts are extremely important for creating your own voice as a librarian or as a group that runs bibliotherapy-adjacent programs!
- *Bonus content:* Image collections and picture galleries provide a great opportunity to reuse content, both text and image, for other mental health–related topics.

Creating Synergies: Putting It All Together

With diminishing resources and staff in the library world, there's no need to explain the benefits of creating synergies. Social media marketing is itself a prime example, as well as an opportunity! Your staff may want to brainstorm about marketing content and strategies that will play off each other on the various platforms. Start with selecting and setting up your social media outlets strategically, based on your program's goals and the library's mission and existing channels, and connect the accounts as the next step. Remember, no matter which platforms you choose, consider their individual characteristics and use them for what they can do the best to market your program, each complementing the others.

A critical element in promoting your bibliotherapy-related programs is the synergy between the content—that is, your reading material, the discussions, and events, as well as your marketing strategies. Social media platforms are powerful on their own merits and also perfect for building on each other, as the examples above indicate.

A popular approach to creating synergies is to promote a program that's already marketed on the website or in a blog post, simultaneously posting about via all social media channels using a distinctive visual cue for branding—a classic example of piggybacking wherever possible. On the flip side, you'll also want to keep a look out for opportunities to make unique posts on each platform that are responsive to its culture and current trends; for example, finding out about a bibliotherapy-adjacent topic that your YouTube users are interested in and responding with a video. User-generated content can also create new opportunities to engage. All of these can be alternated or can complement each other.

MARKETING EXAMPLE

"Author Talks," a Guest Author Event

The moment we find out that our guest author has confirmed the date, we usually share the information in a hold-the-date message. This is communicated widely on diverse channels, such as sending out an email blast, posting on social media, and sharing the date on the website. By the time we're advertising, obviously, we've gathered a lot of content, since our author preselection procedures will have included creating an author profile. These profiles are nothing fancy; in a plain Word document, we simply collect major resources related to the author such as biographical sketches, information from the author's website, a list of publications with links to the title in the catalog, if possible, images and videos of the author, and social media profiles and mentions, with hyperlinks. By the time the first event-related post has to be created, we always have plenty of information.

Sending out the event registration link is usually the next step. The invitation with the form includes a part where participants can list topics and questions that they would like the author to talk about. Along with what we've learned about the author, these responses help inspire bloggers to write posts both before and after the event, which provides an opportunity to connect with participants and makes clear that we're listening to what they say.

The collected content can also be reused in multiple ways, such as on the library homepage, on the event page—even in a LibGuide, if we have a chance to create one. Additionally, QR codes displayed on print material such as flyers, posters, bookmarks, handouts, and banners can also point to the existing event as well as upcoming Author Talks events.

TABLE 10.1

Promotion Tips: Traditional and Social Media

TO-DO LIST	NOTES
When	
Start your promotion as soon as date locked	Delegate, automate, schedule, piggyback
Add on to general library promotional opportunities	
Set up media presence, venues, accounts, access, promo schedule	Keep it simple
	Remember privacy issues
Add to event calendar ASAP on the library website	Create a template with basic plan/language that's welcoming and inclusive
Set up the registration process	Online, secure, fee-based or free, capped, waitlist
Where	
Library physical locations: entrance, circulation desk, public computers	Sensitive topics
Social media: Facebook, Instagram, X (formerly Twitter), blogrolls	Match to audience
	Recruit potential participants to help
Word of mouth: speak up everywhere! (shameless self-promotion)	Success of a program leads to success of the next one

TO-DO LIST	NOTES
What	
Create inventory of social media post types: news, teaser, lead post, content, reminder, recap, group post	Match to audience, topic, and platform Use specific but inclusive language
Explore topics for blog posts: announcement, details about the program, reading suggestions, bibliotherapy benefits	A great chance to share relevant and meaningful content on social media

In a Nutshell

Adding social media to your heavy workload might be the last thing you think you want to do. But if you think social media is purely a waste of time, you may want to look around in the business world: everyone has harnessed the power of one or more platforms for the benefit of their customers, products, and company. Social media means work. Figuring out the best channels for your program will require time and effort. If you try translating some of the suggestions in this chapter to your setting and add relevant library content (don't be afraid to go a bit personal!), you will create your own brand in no time, and it will have a great overall impact on your program.

11 | Improving and Sustaining Your Program

So you've gotten started, and your program is a success . . . but with a few hitches. Or you've presented a single large event with great turnout, but you're not sure how to ride the momentum. How do you make your bibliotherapy-inspired program both adaptive and sustainable? This chapter will discuss how to lay the groundwork for future success while implementing your first events, through continuous assessment and the creation of reusable templates. First, in order to know whether your program is resonating with its intended audience and synergizing with other library programs, you'll need to set SMART (specific, measurable, attainable, relevant, and timely) goals and collect both quantitative and qualitative data on whether you're meeting them. Assessment informs an approach we call *perpetual beta*: paying attention to what is and isn't working and tweaking your program from one iteration to another. We suggest careful documentation and, when things are working, creation of templates to ensure that you can replicate your successes.

Define Your Goals

You can assess whether you have reached your goals only if you have goals in the first place! Assessment starts with asking the right questions, including some difficult ones:

- Are we doing the best we can to serve our community?
- Are we aligned with the mission of the library?

AT A GLANCE

- Define Your Goals
- Are You SMART?
- What Should You Assess?
- What Tools to Use?
- Assess Your Additional Workload
- Perpetual Beta
- Documentation and Templates

- Are we following DEI (diversity, equity, and inclusion) principles in practice?
- Do our numbers add up?
- Are we adding value to the library services?

And the big questions:

- What are our specific goals with our bibliotherapy-infused programs?
- Is there a better or more efficient way to accomplish our goals?
- How do we know when our goal is accomplished?

To assess your program, you need a clear, well-defined goal that provides direction, motivation, and focus. Deciding on the goals for your program may also provide an opportunity to reflect further on larger goals of the library: connecting patrons to information, resources, and support; furthering a sense of community; and so on. One of the great things about bibliotherapy as a framework is that it refocuses our attention on the reasons our users read, and what they might be getting out of reading, in a way that can deepen libraries' own understanding of their mission—not just connecting users to information, for example, but facilitating meaningful reading experiences.

Are You SMART?

The next few paragraphs will help you narrow down your goals of your bibliotherapy project and disambiguate the goal statement. Assessment strategies should incorporate SMART goals—again, objectives you create that are:

- specific
- measurable
- attainable
- relevant
- timely

Specific

A bibliotherapy-related program already represents a rather specific area even in a library: promoting reading for therapeutic purposes through reflection and discussions. Accordingly, your goal statement should be specific, with a clearly defined desired outcome. A vague or tautological goal such as "I want to run a successful bibliotherapy program" is unhelpful, since the whole task of goal setting is to define what success means in the specific context of your program so that you can work toward achieving it.

To work toward an explicit goal statement, you can start with something like "to set up a new reading program for young adults using YA fiction to discuss stress and anxiety in partnership with other wellness initiatives in the community." This goal names the major characteristics of the program (such as relying on existing resources and targeting a specific audience and therapeutic concern), and it ties the program to the local community, its needs, and its initiatives. This goal has the potential to forge new partnerships while remaining within the realm of the library. It also suggests a complementary, rather than competitive, relationship to existing programs in the library and community—an important question to decide early on, before misunderstandings between partners can arise.

Measurable

Any accomplishment that can be observed and/or charted counts as measurable—think circulation data, attendee numbers, and website visits. Measuring progress with predefined, consistent criteria and data-collection systems will indicate if your bibliotherapy-infused project is on track or any adjustments are needed. Social media platforms and websites are conducive to assessment, as long as they already fit the profile of your program. For example, for a reading program geared toward teens, social media would be a great way to collect statistical data such as page views, reaches, impressions, shares, and likes. However, for a more substantial assessment, more traditional methods such as event attendance or circulation statistics should also be considered.

Here are some examples of measurable outcomes for a one-year period of our hypothetical project, a YA-targeted program addressing stress and anxiety:

- **Circulation:** Increase circulation count of related YA titles by 10 percent.
- **Events:** Host ten book club discussions and two author events.
- **Social media:** Increase the number of followers by 35 percent; achieve a reach average of 500 followers/post; add one new social media outlet to the existing ones.

You can add measurable benchmarks to your original goal: "via monthly Zoom book discussions and related follow-up on social media" or "to increase the circulation of YA titles by 10 percent."

Attainable

For your goals to remain realistic and achievable, but still challenging, you will need to do your homework first and explore your resources. A good synonym for *attainable* might be "within reach," and it can be helpful to think of that literally: What can you do with the resources that are already in your library? Bibliotherapy-centered projects are great for setting attainable goals because they rely on available resources: high-quality reading material and talented, literate staff. Keep in mind, though, that while your goal should be attainable, it should also be at least a bit of a challenge—enough to inspire and motivate you and your team to stretch yourselves. Aiming too high or too low can defeat the purpose of setting your goal in the first place.

For example, if the program targets one specific audience for a start— say, young adults—do you have someone who can act credibly as the face of the program? Someone knowledgeable, relatable, and authentic? Does the library have the desired reading material in the collection? If you pick a certain title, does the library have enough copies or unlimited online access? Do you have the expertise in the library to run a book club? Moderate discussions? Host a guest author? Are you confident you can reach your audience in time for a successful turnout? Do you have the skills to make sure that your marketing strategies work toward your success? Do you have buy-in from your users? From your colleagues? From management?

Relevant

Not only is a relevant goal significant and results oriented, but it also aligns with the library's broader goals and visions. Tailored properly to the library's mission, a bibliotherapy-focused activity is likely to have a great impact if it is designed with a relevant goal in mind. Considering programs with a potentially high yield (aka the best bang for your buck), in the planning phase will make a real difference for your library and your community. From time to time, it's worth revisiting the relevance of your goal and even setting up reminders of why you made this choice.

For example, if the goal is to address stress and anxiety among teens, you would want to be sure that this is a pressing concern in the community. If it is, there may be potential partners out there already addressing it—school counselors, for example, or parent groups. To decide whether a goal is relevant, in the planning phase, it's worth casting a wide net and capitalizing on existing reports and analyses to learn from running programs and their success stories. Again, librarians are often already familiar with the issues facing their communities, and anecdotal evidence from library staff, users, and community members should also be considered.

Timely

Setting benchmarks or phases for your project will keep you on track to accomplish its original goals. Other than the obvious starting and ending date marking the duration of the program (such as the school year or summer break), a realistic timeline with built-in deadlines and milestones is useful for any project, with or without a fancy project-management tool. A timeframe is also important for keeping your staff on the same page—especially crucial if your staff includes different working styles, multiple locations, or hybrid work arrangements. Timing helps set priorities, short and long term. A detailed timeline will keep everyone focused by prompting action when necessary, supporting the completion of deadlines at a manageable pace. It can also reduce general anxiety, as participants will have to focus on the next, manageable item on the timeline.

An example of a SMART goal for a bibliotherapy program might sound like: In the 2023/24 school year, increase our circulation of YA books by 15 percent via biweekly in-person reading groups and monthly new arrivals lists with staff picks, reaching out to high school students, parents, and counselors.

PERFORMANCE INDICATORS

Love your numbers! Assessment also motivates performance. Just as you might derive inspiration from tracking your personal fitness goals—digging a little deeper for a personal best in the weight room or feeling that sense of accomplishment from hitting ten thousand steps—metrics can motivate you and your team to stick with your bibliotherapy-based project in difficult times by providing milestones to celebrate and continuous diagnostic feedback to improve. Choosing to share your results with interested parties on the library's homepage or in the library newsletter, internal or external, also maintains a certain level of accountability. The weekly internal newsletter of the Rutgers University–New Brunswick Libraries, *Our Stories*, had a column called "Assessment Moment of the Week," providing a venue for short write-ups with statistics combined with any other qualitative assessments, aka impact stories. The five-hundred-word-maximum articles typically included infometrics and served multiple functions: documenting the process of projects, telling a story, contributing to the larger picture of the libraries, informing stakeholders and colleagues, and (last but not least!) holding project participants accountable. These mini-assessments could also provide great draft material for marketing communications and final reports.

What Should You Assess?

Time consuming as it is, assessment conducted continuously or at multiple points will provide plenty of data over time and will serve as a powerful component to justify or expand your project. Here are a few additional points to consider:

- The assessment timeline should match the project timeline as closely as possible, with perhaps just a slight delay.
- Collecting data from different platforms, one at a time, allows librarians to set up comparison charts and monitor trends from different angles.

- Low-hanging fruit includes frequently used measures such as OPAC circulation numbers, attendance at programs, website visits, and number of media stories or media mentions.
- Set up a "brag sheets" folder for word-of-mouth feedback, letters of appreciation, or any awards and honors received.
- Existing assessment tools such as Springshare products can also be used for assessment purposes. For example, setting up a "bibliotherapy" tag for related reference questions in the reference assessment tool can indicate specific interest and how it changes over time.
- Each social media platform has its own assessment tool, with some even allowing for some customization. Engagement can be assessed via a whole slew of measures, such as impressions, link clicks, number of comments, number of followers, reach, saves, shares, and views. Given the disappearing nature of these reports (sometimes the last month or last 90 days only), it's advisable to save brief summaries of basic social media metrics so you can properly monitor trends and see what worked and what didn't.
- Social media platforms can also give a hint about the best time to publish, considering your specific topic and audiences.

Again, assessment is time consuming, and monitoring various platforms only adds to the workload, especially if you're trying to do it consistently (as it should be done). However, librarians are used to benefiting from automation in many other areas in their work. You can get inventive automating many applications in assessment too!

What Tools to Use?

Assessment tools collect several useful metrics that provide outstanding feedback on the actual use of the content. For example, for your website: if the library already subscribes to a fee-based service, such as one of the Hootsuite products, it's relatively easy to add the bibliotherapy program's various web and social media components. Another service is the free tool Google Analytics, which allows website owners to see patterns in user interaction. Whatever you decide to use, data collection shouldn't happen for the sake of just collecting data but should focus on how to make sense of the collected data to improve your program.

What Data?

For websites, in addition to basics such as total number of page views ranked by most frequently visited pages, you can get to know your users better with demographic data, including language and geographical location—incredibly useful metrics to assess a bibliotherapy-inspired program to find out if you've reached your target audience. You can analyze which social media platforms drive the most traffic to your site, how long your visitors stayed on the pages, how many (if any) more pages they clicked on, and what the final page they viewed was.

As for more complex assessment measures, you can also track what kind of content or which pages are visited most frequently. An interesting way to take a combination of quantitative and qualitative measures is to follow individual pages over time. You may discover that certain perennial or sensitive topics tend to increase page views over time, or at a certain time of the year (such as topics on mental health around major holidays), even if they didn't perform very well at the beginning. These insights can be

---

FIGURE 11.1
Sample statistics

Chang Science Library
BOOKS WE READ

| **18,996** | **47,385** | **25,078** |
| visitors | page views | sessions |

| **89** | **291** | **1,292** |
| pages | blog posts | images |

Data: 3/1/2020 - 2/28/2023 (Google Analytics)
go.rutgers.edu/booksweread

used not only to document use over time but also for long-term marketing, either by reusing and relinking popular bibliotherapy-inspired content or creating similar ones.

Anecdotal Evidence

You should never underestimate the power of word-of-mouth assessment. Combined with hard data, any evidence you can amass from one-on-one conversations (taking confidentiality into account, of course), comments on social media platforms, feedback during a public event, and a review of photo documentation will help you develop your narrative as you write your stories of impact.

In addition to external media mentions, you may want to harvest social media for any program-related photos or videos that appear on other social media coverage. A quick reminder: if you didn't think of setting up boundaries about who can take photos at your public events, you may want to write up or update your policies, including creating and using a media release form consistent with your library's policies. The same applies to recording events at the library or online.

WHAT IS AN IMPACT STORY?

Telling your story is a great way to engage your audience. An impact story is similar to a case study, but more conversational: a structured presentation of your program and what it has achieved, mixing anecdotal and quantitative data in an approachable, engaging manner. Impact stories put a face on your program, and they're particularly appropriate for bibliotherapy-related projects; a big part of bibliotherapy, after all, hinges on the way that stories can connect with their audiences.

There are many ways to write an impact story. You can focus on a single event, person, or book, you can lead with either your data or your program's origin story—whatever seems most engaging to you. Just make sure to keep the tone light and conversational,

and to illustrate how your program facilitates therapeutic, transformative encounters with texts for your program's participants.
Odds are your listeners will be able to relate to that kind of reading
experience.

Assess Your Additional Workload

Last but not least, assess the staff time your event or program used, broken
down to librarian/staff/volunteer groups and assignments. Bibliotherapy-infused tasks seem to have their own rabbit holes! Although a proper
return on investment would be rather difficult to compute, changes in staff
involvement in the project should be documented to avoid an excessive
investment of human resources and to justify the sometimes out-of-the-
ordinary tasks a bibliotherapy-related project might involve.

Periodically, it's worth reviewing each strategy from an HR investment
angle. Perhaps it will give you an answer why something did or didn't work.
Then, combining these findings with other assessment strategies and using
what you learned in making future marketing and communications plans,
and programming, you can pick and choose to benefit from assessment
as a general tool for any project, including your next bibliotherapy group.

ASK THE EXPERT

WILLIAM BEJARANO
The Assessment Funnel

William Bejarano is a PhD candidate at the School of Communication
and Information at Rutgers University–New Brunswick.

A helpful heuristic to use when assessing a service or program
is to picture an inverted pyramid or funnel, tapering down from
broad theoretical ideas to more specific day-to-day decisions and
applications. At the broad end, one first ought to consider just

what is meant by value; that is, before any specific assessment decisions are made, there needs to be a clear understanding of an institution's general mission statement and its intended purpose. This can and should be summarized in a literal statement no more than a few sentences long that is specific enough to guide day-to-day decisions, but general enough to provide flexibility in implementing those decisions.

Descending down the funnel, it is important to note the context of the particular time, place, and culture in which a program is being implemented by reviewing the different stakeholders and various perspectives both from "above" (e.g., governments, public and private funding bodies, administrators) and "below" (e.g., the library users or community members being served). As you narrow down, you can then devise plans and review or develop models to collect data relevant to the mission statement in this particular context.

Further down comes decisions on the strategies and techniques that should be used to measure and analyze metrics, as well as provide comparisons—with the same program at a different point in time, with similar institutions, or with a set standard benchmark. Finally, at the very bottom of the funnel are decisions to be made regarding whether and how to adjust the program in future iterations. These can be presented as periodic reports or more real-time dashboards accessible to the audiences that were highlighted earlier.

Applying this funneling technique to the topic of bibliotherapy, the anticipated value of such a program could be summarized by a mission statement that reads something like: "Our program's mission is to curate and disseminate books appropriate for helping those with a variety of ailments, disorders, or general problems." The groups to be considered stakeholders in this program depend on who the constituencies for your library are. If the program is being implemented in a public library, for instance, the target audiences from "above" could be local policymakers, funding bodies, or philanthropists, and "below" would be the general audience of those who may be helped by the anticipated collection, as well as their friends and families. Given this mission, in this context, decisions can be made about what ought to be measured and how to do it.

Some preliminary data can be established by using personal techniques (i.e., surveys, interviews, and/or focus groups) to establish a baseline level of the "ailments, disorders, and general problems" that are felt by the intended audience, as well as preliminary ideas about reading and their thoughts on the potential for this service. The same measures as well as new measures can then be implemented at different points over the course of the program to gauge the impact of the program qualitatively and/or quantitatively, effectively measuring the service against itself over time. Alternatively, measurements can be compared with similar programs at other libraries if those data are publicly available. Impersonal techniques (e.g., data tracing) can also be used to determine the popularity of the service—web analytics, attendance numbers, repeat patrons, or other quantifiable measures.

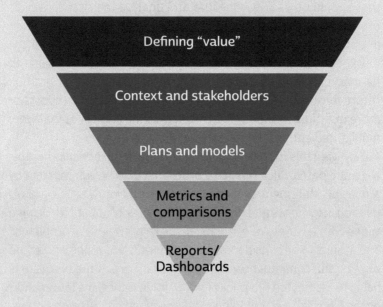

Perpetual Beta

Just as assessment is not a single moment but an ongoing process that should happen throughout your program, improving your program doesn't have to be a complete and sudden overhaul. Instead, you can fine-tune and tweak from one iteration of your program to the next, or even between sessions of an ongoing program. In order to keep your program nimble and adaptive, we recommend an approach we call *perpetual beta*, in which each session, event, or iteration of the program is a sort of trial run for the next. This doesn't have to be exhausting; it's simply a way to make sure that you're processing the valuable experience you collect when running a program. What worked, and what didn't? What might you do differently or similarly next time? Minor course corrections add up, preventing the need for an about-face later—and participants are typically glad to see that you're open to feedback and dedicated to improvement.

This process of iterative improvement can start before you even launch: Why not test your hypothetical program in a mock environment? Between group discussions, online resources, live events, and so on, a bibliotherapy program can have a lot of moving parts, not to mention dealing with sensitive topics that require careful handling. Aware of what to expect and ready to troubleshoot if (or realistically, when) things go wrong, you will feel more confident entering a live public event, for example, if you've already tested it with in-house users (think staff members, student workers, and library volunteers).

Testing the waters with brand-new or existing content, be they texts, images, or templates, will help prepare you for some of the most obvious issues that might come up. For marketing and assessment, you may want to develop a basic but flexible inventory of tools to use on the fly during your first few programs, testing them in various settings for different purposes. You don't want to have to figure out a procedure for setting up a social media schedule all over again for each platform!

Of course, there will always be some adjustments as you coordinate the different parts of your project across the different working styles and schedules of your team. Extending the planning phase (but not too long) and testing ideas in-house has worked well for us. It gives us plenty of time to brainstorm, do our homework and due diligence, gather information, compare notes, come up with different scenarios, and write up a first draft of your plan. After a few rounds of discussing, analyzing, overanalyzing, and agonizing over what can go wrong, we manage to reach a consensus that leaves us 90 percent satisfied—leaving some questions open and some issues unresolved, but preparing us with backup plans and giving us confidence in our ability to improvise given our preparation, data, and instincts. Once we had a few successful bibliotherapy-inspired projects and events, we arrived at a point where we also trusted our experience. "Good enough" was good enough.

Documentation and Templates

Even if you are proficient in programing, you already know that accidents do happen. Additionally, bibliotherapy-based programs come with a new level of anxiety for all parties. We all make mistakes; technology fails; last-minute changes are inevitable sometimes; and the jitters you get from walking into a classroom with forty students never go away (just ask any classroom teacher or librarian). We always start a program, whether in person or online, ready with a backup plan based on a proven template.

Templates also help you preserve what has worked in the past. As you work on your first program, try converting your materials—discussion sheets, event playbooks, marketing communications, and data-collection forms—into reusable templates. You're even welcome to adapt some of the examples we offer in this book for your own purposes! Across the different facets of your program, templates are the most concrete way to leverage what you've learned to make the subsequent iterations go smoothly.

No matter what you choose to reuse or tweak from one program to another, we'll leave you with the most basic and important advice for assessment and sustainability: documentation, documentation, documentation! Keep written, well-organized, easy-to-find records of what you have done and how it has or hasn't worked. Doing so will provide a more accurate depiction of your program's track record and areas for growth, and it will save you a great deal of time and labor that would otherwise be spent reinventing the wheel. Your future self will thank you.

Not only will your future self thank you for documenting your work, in fact, but so will future team members who may not be on the project now. The impact of your program is tied directly to its sustainability and replicability—whether it can be implemented in the future, once original team members (perhaps including you) have moved on, or by another team in another location. Think of all the documentation you do, however minor, as a kind of trailblazing for others yet to come. If you plan your bibliotherapy program well, it can be a part of your legacy, touching future generations of readers, as future teams of librarians follow in your footsteps—but only if they can follow your notes!

In a Nutshell

Your bibliotherapy-based project can always get better. Taking a "perpetual beta" approach helps you collect relevant data to assess how your program is reaching audiences and meeting their needs, and repeat what worked or change what didn't. It all starts with SMART (specific, measurable, attainable, relevant, and timely) goals that organize your overall mission into more discrete benchmarks in order to assess your progress. Both quantitative and qualitative data can help you evaluate your program and see what needs improvement. Last but certainly not least, make sure to document every step of the process! Careful documentation can help you troubleshoot when problems arise (as they often do in unpredictable live events), reuse what works rather than reinvent the wheel, and leave a sustainable, replicable blueprint in place that new teams can follow, either at other libraries or once you and your staff have moved on.

EPILOGUE
New Directions: Looking Forward

So you've gone through the whole process and brought your bib-liotherapy-inspired library program to fruition. You've celebrated your successes, learned from your mistakes, and collected some helpful feedback. What comes next? This chapter will explore some ideas to build on your success further and expand your program into new areas. We'll discuss how to incorporate bibliotherapy into more areas of your library and how to supplement your guided reading program with new activities such as creative writing and art. This is the time to leave the beaten track for uncharted territory; this chapter will point out some possible trailheads for you to explore. Your program doesn't need to stop growing, and neither do you in your rewarding journey as an intentional "accidental bibliotherapist."

Adding Creativity and Play

Has encountering someone else's work ever inspired you to create something of your own? The transition from guided reading to creative practice is a natural next step for your bibliotherapy program too. Storytelling and creative writing are easy places to start. You might also consider having participants create visual art (produced as analog or digitally), either as illustrations for the texts you read or as standalone works. If you have a blog, you can even showcase participants' work there! Content created by participants is the gift that keeps on giving: it's a rewarding experience for the creators and a powerful testament to what

> ### AT A GLANCE
>
> - Adding Creativity and Play
> - Creative Writing and Storytelling: In Their Own (Six) Words
> - Combining Methods of Bibliotherapy Creatively
> - Sketching and Visual Arts
> - Teaching Library Research Skills with Bibliotherapy in Mind
> - One More for the Road: Bibliotherapy for Your Own Growth

they're getting out of your program—for yourself, for library decision makers or funders, and for potential future participants.

SAMPLE CREATIVE ADD-ONS

- Creative writing, storytelling, and blogging
- Sketching and graphic design
- Creating social media content

You might as well combine several creative elements and try adding a creative contest to your program. There's nothing better to challenge your readers than inviting them to express their relationship to a text via their creative products such as blog posts, images, or even TikTok videos. Books today exist in an ongoing relationship with reader feedback and reader-generated content, and your program can deepen participants' relationships with what they read. At a minimum, these add-on activities will reach out to more people and will help forge new alliances in your community. The examples in this book illustrate how a bibliotherapy-based program can quickly be adapted to new needs and circumstances (including a once-in-a-lifetime pandemic).

The best place to start, as usual, is with the expertise you have in-house. For example, we've benefited from team members with artistic gifts: a student worker with a talent for drawing provided illustrations for therapeutic reading material, a graduate assistant created a booktalk video to interpret a short story, and an art librarian helped us in a number of ways, from being the judge for our creative art contests to sponsoring artistic events to illustrating this book (thanks, Megan C. Lotts!). Draw on the skills and passions of your team members, be willing to think outside the box, and you'll often find that participants are eager to follow. Enthusiasm is contagious!

Creative Writing and Storytelling:
In Their Own (Six) Words

Not only is reading a helpful, potentially therapeutic way of processing one's experience—writing and storytelling can be too. Consider adding a fiction or nonfiction creative writing component to your program. The field of addictions (the area where our own engagement with bibliotherapy first originated) has developed its own strong storytelling traditions—think of the stories told in a twelve-step meeting, for instance. Hearing the stories of others helps participants feel less alone in their struggles. And the simple act of telling a story has further therapeutic value: bringing one's shame and demons out into the light, sorting through difficult experiences to make meaning out of them, seeing a bigger picture, and taking the power to rewrite one's own ending.

Addiction-related storytelling taught us that stories don't necessarily have to be artfully developed or lengthy to make a powerful, inspirational read. Short narratives—as short as Ernest Hemingway's famous six words ("For Sale: baby shoes, never worn.")—might possess emotional depth and can provoke thoughts and insights. Why not try a six-word-story contest? If you have a blog, you can even showcase participants' work there! (With their permission, of course.)

A low-key in-house project promoted as a stressbuster at the library featured a simple posterboard set up by the entrance encouraging students to take a break and add their six-word flash fiction. Students saw the display on their way into the library and were hesitant at first about what to do, just stopping to read the examples our library student workers wrote. Once a few brave souls posted their stories, the board soon filled up and a new one was necessary in a few days. The six-word stories uncovered students' states of mind, from anxiety to hope and anything in between.

Combining Methods of Bibliotherapy Creatively

In the middle of the COVID-19 pandemic, the practicing bibliotherapist Viktória Tóth founded an online mixed-methods bibliotherapy group for a very specialized audience: Hungarians living abroad. During a time when everyone was dealing with different kinds and aspects of isolation, the group hoped to offer new forms of connection based on a shared experience. Notably, Tóth—a native of Hungary now based out of Finland—has participants write as well as read texts, in what she calls a blend of Finnish "active" (or writing-oriented) bibliotherapy with Hungarian "receptive" (or reading-oriented) methods. Tóth was gracious enough to share her insights below.

ASK THE EXPERT

VIKTÓRIA TÓTH
On the Road

Viktória Tóth is a bibliotherapist in Finland.

My On the Road online bibliotherapy groups are aimed at Hungarian expats living permanently abroad, and the main goal is to use the methods of developmental bibliotherapy to address concerns related to integration in their new homes.

Finnish bibliotherapists mostly use what's called "active bibliotherapy," or writing therapy, in which sessions usually focus on texts written by the participants themselves. Hungarian bibliotherapists, by contrast, typically practice "receptive bibliotherapy," in which sessions focus on already-published texts; creative or therapeutic writing plays only a supporting role (if any). My aim is to use both methods to create a more intensive experience for participants, so they get writing tasks during the sessions and between the sessions also.

We work with short and extremely varied texts. There are classical and contemporary Hungarian literature, prose, short stories, poems, also short citates, tales, songs but also silent books, pictures, and objects. Additionally, participants have the opportunity to recommend texts for others. There is a sort of thematic arc to the group sessions, but I will often adjust it according to a particular group's interests and concerns.

The groups meet six times, for a total of twelve hours together—a short but intensive experience. Typical topics are related to the contrast between the old and new identities, feelings of otherness and uncertainty, challenges of work and family life, understanding of the mechanisms of the culture, fears of making decisions, and so on. Sometimes small things—like the pronunciation of our names abroad—are hiding big questions. Often we discuss and process our relationships to our home country, to the Hungarian communities in our new homes, and to relatives and friends back in Hungary.

The feedback from participants is very positive: they find a supportive small community in these groups. Using the Hungarian language and returning to their roots through Hungarian literature make sessions feel familiar and welcoming to participants. Participants share a great deal of themselves in the group and come to know themselves better in the process—they are taking risks in a safe, supportive, and constructive environment.

Sketching and Visual Arts

In addition to creative writing, you can consider a creative component that involves a different kind of art altogether. They say a picture is worth a thousand words; if you have an artist on your team, perhaps you could add a drawing or other visual arts component to your program.

ASK THE EXPERT

MEGAN C. LOTTS
What Is Urban Sketching?

Megan C. Lotts is the art librarian at Rutgers, the State University of New Jersey.

Urban sketching is a movement created in 2007 by Seattle journalist and illustrator Gabriel Campanario, encouraging the drawing of spaces and places on location, rather than drawing from photographs. The goal is simple: sketch what you see, in- or outdoors, and share it online. It's diverse and inclusive, bringing together an international group of people who "show their world one drawing at a time." The best part: you don't need to be an artist, an expert, or even someone who draws all the time!

Using the hashtag #rutgersurbansketching, it is now a tradition at Rutgers to dedicate the month of November to walking around campus and sketching, with or without weekly prompts or instructions. Workshops are open to anyone who wants to try urban sketching.

There can be a real therapeutic benefit to urban sketching. Members of our community are looking for activities to help them connect with each other and share their experience. Sketching scenes from daily life encourages mindfulness and elevates seemingly mundane moments, allowing us to see our own world from a different perspective. It relieves stress, hones observational and analytical skills, and forces us to take a moment to stop and "draw the roses."

Teaching Library Research Skills with Bibliotherapy in Mind

If you work at a school or university library, you might also find ways to incorporate ideas from bibliotherapy into your library education efforts. When teaching students how to find or cite books, you might add more depth to the exercise by asking them to choose a book that spoke to them or helped them at a particular moment in their lives, and to share that experience. (Whether students will share with the whole class or only with you is up to them, but make sure to be clear about which it is up front.) Even reluctant readers are likely to have at least one book that has meant something to them, and this storytelling exercise can remind students of all the things reading can do outside of research, even as they learn valuable research skills. Perhaps they'll even be inspired to check out their peers' selections!

FIGURE E.1

The iconic bridge at the Rutgers Center of Alcohol Studies connects library users and resources

Source: Sketch by Megan C. Lotts

ASK THE EXPERT

JUDIT H. WARD
When a Poster Tells a Thousand Words

When library resources are introduced to first-year students at the Chang Science Library, the class activity at the end of the session is designed for them to put what they learned that day into practice by creating a book poster: to choose a book that had spoken to them that they would recommend to fellow students. This librarian-directed, fifteen-minute activity serves multiple purposes: figuring out how to search for materials, getting used to bibliographic records and how to save them, creating a mini-poster with proper citation and credits, and most of all providing peer-to-peer recommendations for books that have proven meaningful for our students.

The exercise has resulted in hundreds of posters over the years—perfect for an in-house exhibit or virtual browsing when added to online poster galleries. The mini-posters have been exhibited across four different libraries on campus. These exhibits provide a wonderful backdrop for events, showcasing elements of the library collection. And they're a fun way to teach students about how to navigate the library. More important, they remind the students who make them and anyone who looks at them of the power of reading to counsel, to console, and to facilitate growth. There's no recommendation more meaningful than peer to peer, for a specific meaningful book or for the library in general.

One More for the Road: Bibliotherapy for Your Own Growth

This book emphasizes the therapeutic process between the text and the reader. However, you the "accidental bibliotherapist" or event moderator also count as a reader. The text, as well as the process of working on the text with a group, affects you too. A bibliotherapy-centered approach provides an unparalleled opportunity to grow as a professional and as a person. When you click with your audience, their gain is your gain too!

ASK THE EXPERT

NICHOLAS A. ALLRED
Bibliotherapy in the Classroom and Beyond

While I was a PhD student in English at Rutgers, I worked on our bibliotherapy-inspired programs while learning to teach literature classes—effectively, two different kinds of guided reading and discussion. The two reinforced and supplemented each other in sometimes surprising ways.

From the beginning, I wanted to bring approaches from literary studies into our programs. In literary studies, we try to get students to think about how a text works: not just what it's trying to say, but *how* it's trying to say it. I tell my students that I don't want them to focus on uncovering the "message" of the story or poem, as though it were a Christmas present waiting to be extracted from its wrapping paper; instead, the language in which the story presents itself—that wrapping paper—is precisely what we're most interested in and is often the source of the most unexpected insights. (Literature professors can be like toddlers or cats in this respect; the "point" of the story, if there is one, can get boring quickly, but the linguistic package it comes in promises hours of open-ended play!)

Paying attention to how the text says what it says can provide real benefits in a bibliotherapeutic setting, just like in the classroom. Unpacking the language of a text can provide new insights in a way that cutting straight to the "message" generally can't. What's more, talking about literary form provides the kind of indirection that allows participants to sit with difficult issues while controlling their own level of vulnerability.

But while I started by bringing principles from the literature classroom into bibliotherapy programs, I soon found ideas from bibliotherapy informing the way I teach as well. Bibliotherapy has helped me think more deeply about the ways my students identify or engage with texts, not just as scholars but as whole people. Scholarly reading practices are never quite so distant from emotional responses as literary scholars sometimes present them to be; bibliotherapy has helped me see my students' reading in a more complete way, and it has made me a more complete teacher as a result.

On a personal note, the authors of this book benefited tremendously from discussing texts between themselves and with program participants. We connect with these words from Tóth, the seasoned professional bibliotherapist:

For me as a bibliotherapist and as a person who has lived abroad for more than twelve years, my groups are providing a huge learning experience. It is all the time getting clearer and clearer to me that we all are struggling not only with the challenges of living abroad but also—of course—with every other aspect of human life. From this point of view, the name of my group, On the Road, can be understood as symbolic for our whole life as a journey.

We hope that your own journey with bibliotherapy is as rewarding for you and your participants as ours has been.

In a Nutshell

Just like bibliotherapy itself, running a bibliotherapy-inspired program is an ongoing process of learning, developing, and expanding. You as a librarian running these sessions will undoubtedly bring much to the table. Just like us, once you've gotten the hang of it, you will want to experiment with new themes, new audiences, new delivery methods, and new initiatives and collaborations. This chapter has identified areas for extension and exploration, including creative components like writing and visual art; the rest is up to you to discover and make your own. As seasoned bibliotherapists will attest, the process of bibliotherapy can be transformative for the facilitator as well as the participants. You never know what you might discover about yourself too. Keep learning and have fun!

PROGRAM TEMPLATE

Table 3.1 provides a template to plan your bibliotherapy-centered program, including decision points and our tips. The chart below can be used to design your roadmap as you are taking notes during the planning process.

	DECISION POINTS	NOTES
TIME		
Length of program	Semester long? All summer? Shorter duration?	
Frequency	Once a week? Once a month?	
Length of session	60 minutes? 90 minutes? Overtime?	
Schedule	Weekday or weekend? Morning, midday, or evening?	
DELIVERY		
Venue	Onsite or remote? In the library or other physical location?	
AUDIENCE		
	Defined by age group?	
	Special topic? Local flavor/ community interests?	

	DECISION POINTS	NOTES
READING MATERIAL		
Theme and topic	Theme and reading material to select?	
	Length? Accessibility of text (in collection/free online)?	
	Possible challenges?	
Discussion potential	Talking points or questions?	
	Discussion sheets or ad lib?	
MODERATOR/ SPEAKER		
Choice	Moderator(s): librarian or staff member?	
	Previous or new?	
Guest	Guest speaker/author: local or big name?	
	Funding: by the library or cofunded?	

DISCUSSION GUIDE TEMPLATE

F. Scott Fitzgerald: "Sleeping and Waking"

Synopsis

In a first-person, confessional tone, F. Scott Fitzgerald's short story explores chronic insomnia. An unnamed narrator struggles each night to fall asleep. From the mosquito he blames for first disrupting his bedtime routine to the escapist fantasies he uses to try and lull himself to sleep, the narrator draws us in with self-deprecating wit. But as the night goes on, his desperation boils over into a personal crisis, only for him to collapse with exhaustion and wake up to face another day and night of the same. Fitzgerald, a heavy drinker for most of his short life, portrays insomnia as a vicious cycle of self-reproach and oblivion eerily reminiscent of addiction.

The Story

Fitzgerald, F. Scott. "Sleeping and Waking." In *On Booze*, 55–62. New York: New Directions, 2011. Available online by paid subscription in its first published version in *Esquire*, December 1, 1934, http://classic.esquire.com/article/1934/12/1/sleeping-and-waking.

Why Read This Story?

F. Scott Fitzgerald's short piece about insomnia is what we might today call *autofiction*—a story that might or might not be based on his own experience.

Anyone who has dealt with thoughts and anxieties they can't quite keep out of mind (especially in those late hours when there's nothing else to block them out) will feel like it's their experience too.

Discussion Questions

1. Reread the first paragraph. What might be different about each person's insomnia? What might be similar enough that the narrator can make generalizations or hope that readers might recognize their own insomnia in his (as he seems to have with Hemingway's "Now I Lay Me")?
2. Why does the mosquito disrupt the narrator's ability to sleep? Why has the effect of that night lasted?
3. What might it mean for the narrator to regret having "broken myself trying to break what was unbreakable" (61)?
4. What kind of relationship does the narrator seem to have to sleep? What kind of promise does it have for him? What does he crave about it? Is that craving a part of insomnia, a resistance to insomnia, or both?
5. In what context does the drinking come up? Where is it? What does he use it for?
6. Consider the dreams in this story. What are each of them like? What are some of the differences between the dreams the narrator tries to use to fall asleep and the dreams he has once he is finally sleeping?
7. Why might this story be relevant to the process of addiction and recovery? Is insomnia similar to addiction, or potentially connected? How are they similar, and how different? Would sobriety or recovery be like waking, like sleeping, or not exactly like either?

Notes on Discussion

The discussion questions provided here are suggestions. Groups should not feel required to work through them in order or to address all of them. Instead, these questions are meant to solicit observations that can lead to connections. Those connections can be to personal experience; participants should feel free to share if their experiences can help the group get some insight into the topic at hand, since, after all, that's the point of the exercise.

Don't feel compelled to jump to the "point" or "lesson" of the text right away. Philosophically speaking, the text doesn't contain a "lesson"; if anything, the discussion does. Give that discussion time to develop, and make sure participants respond to or build on each other's points rather than jumping around. If you're having trouble getting the ball rolling or finding something insightful to say, try focusing on a particularly complex passage and figuring out what makes it hard to follow or make sense of. Don't be afraid of asking questions you don't know the answer to—articulating a question can be just as valuable to a discussion as providing an answer.

About the Author

Francis Scott Key Fitzgerald (September 24, 1896–December 21, 1940), known professionally as F. Scott Fitzgerald, was an American novelist and short story writer whose works illustrate the Jazz Age. He is widely regarded as one of the greatest American writers of the twentieth century. Fitzgerald is considered a member of the "Lost Generation" of the 1920s. He finished four novels: *This Side of Paradise*, *The Beautiful and Damned*, *The Great Gatsby*, and *Tender Is the Night*. (Source: Wikipedia.)

EVENT PLANNING TEMPLATE

A summary of tables 8.1, 8.2, 8.3, and 8.4, this worksheet can be used as a checklist before, on the day of, and after *each* event. It includes space for your own notes instead of ours in chapter 8.

TIMING	TASK	NOTES
PRE-EVENT		
1 week before	Check if reading material is available (print/online)	
	Send in a mock registration to find dead links, wrong mandatory fields, and other errors	
	Check if moderator is ready	
	Check if guest speaker/author is ready	
	Have playbook ready	
	Check in with tech support	
	Set up access	
	Collect and/or confirm names/titles of anyone who has helped	
	Post about event on social media	
	Write teaser blog post	
	Send out reminders with link	

TIMING	TASK	NOTES
DAY OF		
1 hr. before	Room is ready OR Zoom works Designate a cohost if online	
	Technology: sound check with moderator, guest, and panelists	
	Have playbook ready	
	Agree on transitions and how to signal problems (e.g., text backchannel)	
15 min. before	Open doors OR Zoom room	
5 min. before	Make first welcome announcement ("The event will start soon.")	
At start	Make second welcome announcement Hit RECORD if to be recorded	
	Introduce yourself, speakers, and guests	
	Establish ground rules	
5 min. into event	Moderator/guest: Read text aloud (whole or excerpt)	
10–15 min. into event	Start discussion with a warm-up (nonthreatening) question	
	Follow with questions (6–10) as planned Change planned order if necessary	

TIMING	TASK	NOTES
	Encourage everyone to speak up (if it's an open discussion)	
	Help them respond to each other	
	Let the discussion flow	
10 min. before end	Ask final question, announcing it as last one	
2–3 min. before end	Wrap it up by thanking guests, participants, assistants by name	
At the end	In person: Make sure participants leave in an orderly manner	
	Online: Turn off recording, if applicable	
	In person or online: Save recording in the cloud	
POST-EVENT		
Immediately	Stay until everyone leaves	
	Thank staff and discuss what went well	
Next hours	Send out official thank-you letters if applicable	
Next day	Post event recap and photos on social media	
	Write teaser blog post about include next event	
Next week	Blog about the event	
	Share content if applicable	

EVENT PLAYBOOK TEMPLATE

This checklist-type, plug-and-play template will come in handy on the day of the bibliotherapy event and will serve as a basis for your event playbook. It is designed to be distributed before the event to anyone on center stage (moderator, speaker, author, anyone introducing your event) and to backstage support (IT staff running the online event, marketing and support staff).

BASICS	[AUTHOR], [DATE], [DELIVERY METHOD] (E.G., JAVIER ZAMORA, JUNE 28, 2023, ONLINE)
Event setup	IT department
Panelists (everyone at table or onscreen)	Author: [NAME]—onscreen all the time
	Moderator: [NAME]—onscreen all the time, with audio & video off during [AUTHOR] reading
	Opened by Librarian / Library Rep [NAME]—greeting
	Wrapped up by [NAME] from [PARTNER]—onscreen for last 5 minutes
Audience	[NUMBER OF ATTENDEES] from registration as of [DATE]
Event address	[URL] for attendees; [URL] for panelists (if separate)
TASK	DETAILS
EVENT	[TITLE OF EVENT]
30 min. before	Room opens for testing
10 min. before	Room opens for attendees
Starting screen	[NAMES] (*all panelists*)

BASICS	[AUTHOR], [DATE], [DELIVERY METHOD] (E.G., JAVIER ZAMORA, JUNE 28, 2023, ONLINE)
5 min. before	PRESHOW ANNOUNCEMENT "Good afternoon. [NAME] Library, in partnership with [PARTNER], welcome you to [EVENT NAME] with [AUTHOR]. We will be starting at 4 PM. Please be advised that all attendees will be unable to unmute their camera or their microphone over the course of today's event. We thank you for joining us and will be starting shortly. If you have any issues with hearing the audio during this event, please confirm that your speaker volume is set appropriately and that your audio output device is connected."
At start INTRO and tech announcements (IT staff)	"Good afternoon. [NAME] Library, in partnership with [PARTNER], welcome you to [EVENT NAME] with [AUTHOR]. Please be advised that all attendees will be unable to unmute their camera or their microphone over the course of today's event. Again, we thank you for joining us."
At start	INTRO, WELCOME, AGENDA (1 min. each) General introductions and welcome (by MODERATOR OF EVENT [NAME]): "Welcome to [EVENT NAME] with [AUTHOR]." Introductions, customized to event, author, and audience, ending with: "Turning it over to [Library Director or Librarian]." Welcome from [NAME] Libraries [Library Director or Librarian]: [One-minute welcome, customized to event, author, and audience.] Demote MODERATOR OF EVENT (if different than MODERATOR OF AUTHOR TALK) to attendee as necessary MODERATOR OF AUTHOR TALK: "For the agenda today, after a brief bio about [AUTHOR], we will ask [AUTHOR] to read from [his/her/their] new novel, [*TITLE*]." Read out author bio from discussion sheet, plus something about the selection. Call on [AUTHOR] to read: "I'll turn it over to [AUTHOR] now to read." Mute MODERATOR
Next 5 min.	AUTHOR reads. (5 min.—see selected text at the end, sent to AUTHOR the day before)
Next 5 min.	Unmute MODERATOR, have discussion
45 min.	Conversation with AUTHOR, including questions sent in with registration

BASICS	[AUTHOR], [DATE], [DELIVERY METHOD] (E.G., JAVIER ZAMORA, JUNE 28, 2023, ONLINE)
8–10 min. before end	Last question: "What's a question you're not often asked but would like to answer?"
5 min. before end	Wrap up, thanks [PARTNER—online, promote to panelist] Thank-yous to: AUTHOR, MODERATOR, COHOSTS, IT Also: "Thank you to all our participants! [Something about the success of the main program, library, etc.] "For final words, we'll close with words of advice from [AUTHOR]. [Find relevant quote; use discussion sheet.]"
End	Shutdown: "Thank you for joining us." OUTRO "[XYZ Library], in partnership with [PARTNER], would like to thank everyone who attended [EVENT NAME] with [AUTHOR] today. We will be closing the event shortly. Thank you, and have a great rest of your day."

MARKETING TEMPLATES

The following templates, examples, and descriptions share the types of texts you can easily customize for your email blasts and website. The shorter messages can be posted on your social media sites, with links.

Essential Template 1: Save-the-Date Teaser

Save, modify, and reuse your teaser to spread the word saying something like

> [Teaser / Call to Action]: Join us for our [Program Name] Author Talk with guest speaker [Author Name] as she discusses her award-winning novels and more with moderator [Moderator Name].
>
> [Details]: The event will be held on [date: day, month, year] at [time] at [location or online]. Sponsored by [name of sponsors].
>
> [OPTIONAL: A paragraph about the author, a list of books in the library catalog]

Essential Template 2: Invitation and Registration

The same applies to invitation/registration posts: repeat or paraphrase template 1, adding perhaps a bit more information about the program, and a giant, colorful REGISTER TODAY button with a link to the registration page.

Essential Template 3: Single Event

Up for grabs below is our tried and proven "Single Event Template," printed here as a sample. With some creative editing and replacement of the salient details, it's all yours!

[Teaser]: Poet Natalie Diaz will be virtually coming to [Library Name] for a live Zoom session! Register today!

[Accomplishments/famous for]: Diaz won an American Book Award for her first collection of poems, *When My Brother Was an Aztec*, in 2012, and released her second collection (*Postcolonial Love Poem*) last year to similar rave reviews. She was awarded a MacArthur Foundation genius grant in 2018 and the Pulitzer Prize for Poetry in 2021 for *Postcolonial Love Poem*.

[Relevant bio sketch]:

A Mojave born and raised in the Fort Mojave Indian Village and an enrolled member of the Gila River Indian Tribe, Diaz is known for addressing issues facing Native communities in her poetry, such as racism, poverty, addiction, and especially the conservation of languages and cultures.

[Author's work in your library or in guide]: Interested to find out more about the author? Check out our author guide compiled for the [Name] Book Club in 2021, where "When My Brother Was an Aztec" is one of the featured poems discussed by students taking summer classes.

[Program details]: Meet the author on [date] at [time]. Natalie Diaz will be the guest of the [Name] Book Club.

The event is free and open to the public, but registration is required.

Essential Template 4: Recurring Program

[Teaser]: Summer Tales Book Club is back! Join our fun summer reading program hosted by New Brunswick Libraries and Summer Session. The program will start on June 1, 2021, but students enrolled in the Summer Session at Rutgers can join us any time during the summer.

[Details]: This noncredit course will be delivered via Canvas. Wondering how it works? Curious about the readings? Have doubts why you should read over the summer? Please check out some of the frequently asked questions and our public guide. https://libguides .rutgers.edu/SummerTales2021

[Reading schedule]: The reading schedule is as follows.

[More teaser]: We are also lucky to have two of the authors accepting our invitation! Come and meet Carmen Maria Machado and Natalie Diaz as part of the Summer Tales Reading Club. See more in our current guide. We are looking forward to reading with you!

[Call to Action]: REGISTER TODAY!

Essential Template 5: Blog Types

Yes, it's possible to create blog posts with recurring content and format. Posts such as teasers, invitations, or simple information sharing of other posts come to mind first. Using a "staff picks" tag, post more-substantial book reviews about the text to be discussed, with links to items in the catalog. Another type is a more reflective post related to the topic of discussion or author, allowing the organizers to share a little bit more personal take before or after the live event. (See sample blog types for bibliotherapy-related social media in chapter 10.)

Language and details from these blog posts can be used on social media with a link to the announcement or original post. The social media schedule follows a similar progression, with weekly reminders of reading schedules for longer programs, which can often be tied to a blog post on the discussed text or one of the author's works.

ABOUT THE AUTHORS AND CONTRIBUTORS

JUDIT H. WARD is a science librarian at Rutgers, the State University of New Jersey. In addition to providing reference, teaching library research, and hosting outreach programs, she promotes reading for mental health and wellness. In her previous position as the director of information services at the Rutgers Center of Alcohol Studies, as the recipient of an ALA Carnegie–Whitney Award in 2014, she developed Reading for Recovery, a bibliotherapy-inspired program for people grappling with addiction. She has presented her research and practice related to guided reading from the librarian's perspective both nationally and internationally. She is the author or coauthor of over 150 articles and seven books, including two bibliotherapy readers in her native Hungarian. She received her MLIS from Rutgers, after earning a PhD in linguistics and a master's in English and Hungarian literature and linguistics from the University of Debrecen, Hungary.

NICHOLAS A. ALLRED is Visiting Assistant Professor of English at Fairfield University in Fairfield, Connecticut. He holds a master's in English from Oxford University and a PhD in literatures in English from Rutgers, the State University of New Jersey. His scholarly writing has appeared in *Eighteenth-Century Fiction*, the *Journal of Studies on Alcohol and Drugs*, and the edited collection *Scholarly Milton* (Clemson University Press in association with Liverpool University Press, 2019). While at Rutgers, he collaborated extensively with the Center of Alcohol Studies and Rutgers University Libraries on bibliotherapy-inspired projects and initiatives, including Reading for Recovery—a guided reading program for people with addictions developed with funding from the ALA Carnegie–Whitney Award. He is currently at work on his first academic monograph, on connections between the prehistory of addiction and conceptions of fictional character in eighteenth-century British culture.

WILLIAM BEJARANO (MLIS, MLER), after a decade-plus in academic and research libraries, currently works as a grants facilitator at the Rutgers Cancer Institute while pursuing a doctorate at the Rutgers School of Communication & Information. His current focus is on communication in the formulation and implementation of public health policy.

MEGAN C. LOTTS (MLIS, MFA) is the art librarian at Rutgers, The State University of New Jersey, where she embraces creativity and play when teaching, building collections, and facilitating programming and events across the New Brunswick campuses. In 2021, the American Library Association published her first book, *Advancing a Culture of Creativity in Libraries: Programming and Engagement*. Lotts is working on her second book, *The Playful Library*, forthcoming 2024.

MARIA ORTIZ-MYERS (MI) is a PhD candidate in LIS at the School of Communication and Information, Rutgers University–New Brunswick. Her research interests include information practice, in particular collaborative information interactions. Her dissertation explores how families of transgender youth pursue information. This work highlights the emotional salience of gender-identity information and the information management that marginalized families perform.

DAVID TATE (MA) is an administrative assistant in higher education at Oxford University Press. Before that, he was coordinator and "printer's devil" with the Rutgers Initiative for the Book. His research focused on twentieth-century and contemporary book and institutional histories of literature and medicine. His article "Offprinting Bibliotherapy: Sadie P. Delaney's Interventions in Media Infrastructures" appeared in the fall 2022 issue of the journal *Book History*.

VIKTÓRIA TÓTH (MA) is a practicing bibliotherapist based out of Finland. She has been working as a language teacher for adults with immigrant backgrounds and as a heritage language teacher for children with Hungarian roots. She also coaches peer groups as well as leading creative bibliotherapy groups for Hungarians living abroad.

INDEX

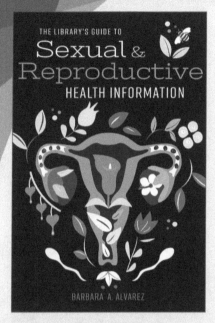
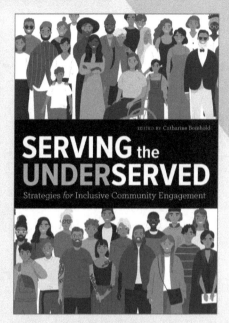
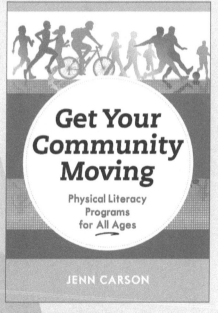